# AMY BIRKS

# THE HUSTLE-Free BUSINESS

## A SIMPLE 7-STEP PLAN
### TO GROW, GET RESULTS, AND HAVE FUN!

NEW YORK

LONDON • NASHVILLE • MELBOURNE • VANCOUVER

# THE HUSTLE-FREE BUSINESS

Published in New York, New York, by Morgan James Publishing in partnership with Difference Press. Morgan James is a trademark of Morgan James, LLC. www.MorganJamesPublishing.com

The Morgan James Speakers Group can bring authors to your live event. For more information or to book an event visit The Morgan James Speakers Group at www.TheMorganJamesSpeakersGroup.com.

ISBN 978-1-68350-422-1 paperback
ISBN 978-1-68350-423-8 eBook
Library of Congress Control Number: 2017901070

**Cover Design by:**
Rachel Lopez

**Interior Design by:**
Megan Whitney
Creative Ninja Designs
megan@creativeninjadesigns.com

In an effort to support local communities, raise awareness and funds, Morgan James Publishing donates a percentage of all book sales for the life of each book to Habitat for Humanity Peninsula and Greater Williamsburg.

Get involved today! Visit
www.MorganJamesBuilds.com

For Tom and August, for being the best
RESULTS I've ever created.

# CONTENTS

# INTRODUCTION

*There is no substitute for hard work."*
*Thomas Edison*

*"While everyone's drinking some damn egg nog,*
*I continue the hustle."*
*Gary Vaynerchuk*

**"I** *just need a plan. Just tell me what the steps are and I'll go do them, OK?"* Her words echoed with familiarity, the look of nervous-excitement on her face almost obligatory for any new client I encounter. We'd been chatting on Zoom, my favorite video-conferencing software, for about 15 minutes before that phrase stumbled out of her mouth. Julie was a money coach. And she, like so many others before her, had a BIG vision for where she wanted to go in her business. She wanted to build her list. She wanted to create passive income from a membership program. She wanted to eventually let go of her one-on-one clients so she could finally have time for the things she loved doing. Her business was moderately successful by her standards, but she wanted to grow. She just had no idea **how** to do it all because it was already so much work just building what she'd already created. But it was when she finally shared her Epic Mission with me that I knew we absolutely had to work together. Julie wanted to change the world.

Does that sound crazy to you? That she wanted to "change the world"? If you've got this book in your hand right now I'm guessing it doesn't. It doesn't sound crazy to me either, by the way. In fact, if a prospective business strategy client **doesn't** want to change the world, they instantly get moved to the "*she's definitely somebody else's client*" category. But not you. You get it.

You, like Julie, have a vision for what's possible in this world. Your business was built on that world-changing vibe. It drives you forward every day and simultaneously overwhelms you at the same time. You're compelled to help others. You're most content when you're serving with your gifts. And although you're already working your little toushie off, you're driven to find a way to do even more to make the world a better place.

And then there's your business. It was supposed to be the vehicle to help you create that change in the world that you want so badly. And to give you the freedom, fun, and fulfillment you've been searching for. But right now, just like Julie, everything feels hard. You're still hustling to find clients even though you've taken all the courses, read all the books, watched all the webinars, and listened to all the podcasts out there that teach everything you need to know about growing your business. You've tried formulas and blueprints and roadmaps and either you kicked your own butt all over creation trying to implement them only to get a moderate result for all that work, or you got completely overwhelmed and threw in the towel before a result could show up. No matter what you try, nothing creates the results you really want and nothing ever feels like "your way." All of this leads to an endless cycle of you working way too hard to generate mediocre results and not getting you any closer to making that big change you want to make in the world.

(How am I doing here? Anything sounding familiar?)

Well, before I take you any further down this path of woe or make you reach for your tissues, let me share what's so awesome about this. (And, of course there's something awesome about this!) What's so awesome about this is that I get it. Completely. I understand what it's like to bust your sweet bottom all the time and wish it didn't have to be so hard. I know what it feels like to be completely confused about what steps to take or strategy to follow to achieve the results you want in your business. I'm acutely familiar with that feeling of overwhelm and discouragement that settles in when you realize that your Epic Mission may just be beyond your capabilities. And I know what it feels like to be *this close* to quitting altogether. That is why I wrote this book.

Over the last three years in my business as The Strategy Ninja, I have encountered entirely too many ridiculously talented coaches just like you who are letting the "hows" of growing their business get in the way of them changing the world. There are too many important missions NOT being acted upon. Too many movements NOT being led. Too many people's lives NOT being impacted for me to not find some way to intervene. You see, I believe that ANYTHING is possible. And that with the right direction, inspiration and support, that can actually be true. We can create that which we most desire. Oh yeah. And it doesn't have to be hard to do it, either.

Don't believe me? Hey, that makes sense. You're stuck in the cycle and used to it being one big hustle. You might even be a loyal disciple in the Church of Chuk. To clarify, that's Gary Vaynerchuk I'm referring to. If you're as well-read and well-studied as I think you are, then you probably know all about the infamous Gary Vee, but if not I'll fill you in. Gary Vaynerchuk is a wildly successful online entrepreneur and the founder of Vayner Media, among other multi-million dollar businesses. He, like me, is extremely passionate about entrepreneurs getting after their dreams and building businesses that will ultimately make an impact in the world. He speaks with zeal and similar frustration about dreamers like us not achieving what we were put on this planet to achieve. It drives him crazy, just like me, that so many talented people out there have something to give and simply aren't serving the world in the biggest way possible. Gary wants everyone to WIN. I admire him immensely and credit him with inspiring so many things related to this book. But... he might be partially responsible for some of that exhaustion and frustration you're feeling right now.

Gary Vee is the king of hustle. He's called hustle *"the most important word ever."* He encourages his fans to *"hustle your face off 15 hours a day to get people to care."* And as much as I love him, I think there's something unsaid, but critically important, within his hustle narrative that the masses who follow him are missing. Our missions are the same, and our philosophies on how to do it are aligned but because his reach is so broad, important details get lost in translation. The critical element that most of his followers tend to miss is this: hustle only feels like hustle when you're working on the **wrong activities**. My intention with this book is to help you identify what the **right** activities are for you so, by the end you'll walk away with a solid strategy for creating the Results That Matter to you without feeling like you're constantly beating yourself up to do it.

And by the way, Gary's not the only one standing up there on the Hustle Your Face Off soapbox. Our culture has been built around this idea that "hard work gets rewarded" and that anyone who's not working hard must be "lazy" or "unsuccessful." Ever heard of the Puritan Work Ethic? That philosophy is the foundation for the American way of life! No wonder so many people think hustle-ness is next to godliness. But while those good old Puritans are pinning a badge of honor on all the 90-hour per week, sleep-when-you're-dead entrepreneurs out there, I know there's a better way.

Because here's the thing. You're hustling, you're hammering away at your goals day in and day out, and you may even be getting results. But here's the kicker. You're not actually enjoying what you're doing if you're hustling. And if you're not enjoying what you're doing, then what's the effing point? You're missing out on precious time doing things that actually matter to you. While you're in your office staring at your laptop till you can't see straight, or hitting every networking event under the sun even though they make you want to drive your car headlong into an oak tree, or you're up till midnight writing your upteenth variation of that email campaign that absolutely-must-go-out-in-the-morning despite the fact that email campaigns are the bane of your existence, there are things happening in your life that you're missing.

Your kids are growing up, making those microscopic changes moment by moment that you just can't get back. The sun shines down on days you would have rather spent at the beach, feet in the sand, listening to the waves crash. Dinners with friends go on without you and your partner starts to forget what you look like. And you're trading all of this for what? To eventually, someday, maybe be able to slow down and enjoy all these things you're missing out on right now? When? At retirement age when you're too old to even enjoy it? Uh, there seems to be a disconnect here.

Let me tell you, that's exactly why I left my cushy corporate job. I couldn't stop thinking about all the LIFE I was missing out on because I had to wait until evenings, weekends, too-short vacations, or even retirement to enjoy them. It's exactly why I started my business and, I'm guessing, probably one of the reasons you started yours too. I can tell you I didn't decide to become an entrepreneur so I could end up feeling as tired as many of those entrepreneurial hustlers I know look most of the time, that's for sure.

So what about you? Why are you still wearing that hustle badge of honor? Isn't it time to take that sucker off and set fire to it for good? Why don't you do that now, actually. I give you permission to just douse it in gasoline and grab a Zippo. I promise it'll be OK if you do. In fact, this book was written to help you feel comfortable doing that. Because I know that giving up the hustle can seem like a Jack-Nicholson-in-The-Shining-crazy thing to do, especially if it's gotten you any sort of results so far. But stay with me here…

You actually **can** work less and still get results. Your business can be filled with ease and fun without worrying that you'll lose the farm. And, in fact, I'll go so far as to say that when you follow the steps outlined in this book, you'll actually get **better results** than you did before, all while dancing on the ashes of your hustle.

Hustling is inefficient at best, and completely spirit-killing at worst. Let's lay yours down once and for all, OK? I managed to do it and haven't ended up bankrupt or homeless or miserable. In fact, quite the contrary. My husband and I moved to the town of our dreams two years ago, we built our business in such a way that he was able to quit his job right before our daughter August was born, so we both get to be home with her all day long. I hop over to the beach when I need to refill my tank in the middle of the day on a Tuesday, and I get to serve amazing clients who do amazing things in the world.

But it wasn't always like this for me. I was a sucker for the hustle myself and even wished I had my own business strategist to tell me how to make things happen. I can distinctly remember using that same familiar phrase Julie used: "*For the love of god, will somebody **please** help me figure out how to run my business successfully and easily???*" It was June, 2013 and I'd just finished getting certified as an Infinite Possibilities Trainer under Mike Dooley (also known as, "The Universe"). Certificate in hand I suddenly realized that no, this piece of paper was not enough to make me a successful business owner.

Still working my full-time corporate gig as a project manager and strategist for a Fortune 25 company, I was under the misguided impression that getting this certification would not only make me credible as a coach - my longtime dream - but it would also magically give me everything I needed to know about how to get clients, make money, and quit my day-job, instantly.

I stood in my living room staring at that piece of paper and suddenly thought, *Hang on a second, I may never actually be able to leave my job after all. I've got to figure this how-to-run-a-business thing out and FAST.* Don't get me wrong, I really liked my job. In fact, most people thought I was crazy to want to leave it, but it just wasn't... enough. It didn't fulfill me like I knew helping people as a business coach would. I wanted more and now that I'd started the train moving with my certification there was no stopping me. So of course I did the first thing I could think of to try and solve this troubling existential dilemma. I checked my Facebook.

This actually ended up not being the total distractionfest it usually is. I'd met a bunch of awesome people at Mike Dooley's conference and got some notifications that some of them wanted to be Facebook friends, so I was exploring their profiles to numb out my confusion about what to do next to actually become an all-growed-up business-owner in real life. One of my new friends had listed on her profile that she had been a student at this weird place called "Marie Forleo's B-School." Intrigued because I'd never heard of it before, I decided to look it up.

When Google directed me to Marie Forleo's website I thought I'd won the lottery. Her B-School program looked like the answer to my prayers. It promised to give me everything I needed to build a successful online business. Her marketing looked slick, the price point was perfect, and the descriptions of the modules were exactly what I was looking for to get my fledgling coaching business off the ground. I looked all over the internet trying to find an opportunity to buy the B-School thing but was dumbfounded when I couldn't find a way to give this Marie Forleo lady my money. I even emailed her team to ask what the deal was. I received a prompt, courteous email back letting me know that I'd *just* missed the window for this year's enrollment in B-School and I'd have to wait until **next** March before they'd launch again and I could join.

Wait, huh? What did she mean they wouldn't sell it to me right now when I needed it? What was this "launch" thing she was talking about anyway? And wait till **March of next year** to get my business off the ground? Was she crazy? I needed help right now! And Marie Forleo was clearly the only person on the planet that could support me on this mission. Being completely green to this whole online business thing, I sent another email or two begging, crying, and cajoling to try and guilt my way into the program 6 weeks after it had already started, but alas I was (of course) unsuccessful in my endeavor. I would have to wait patiently for next March to roll around before I could get my B-School fix. To say I was disappointed would be the understatement of the century.

Even though I couldn't satiate my immediate B-School desire, now my fire was lit. If something as magical as Marie Forleo's program existed, that meant that there had to be other things like it out there in the world to help show me the way. And so like every good online coach does, I signed up for every tool, every list, every freebie, every webinar, and every course under $1,000 under the sun. If there was a 7-Day List-Building/Instagram/Twitter/ Video Marketing Challenge out there, you'd better believe I was in. I had no idea why I needed any of these tactics yet, but it seemed utterly critical to join each Challenge, so I couldn't wait to dive in and learn.

And dive in and learn I did. By the end of that summer I'd amassed an enormous knowledge base about online marketing. I knew the ins and outs of all the best tactics, from pre-sale strategies to 8-figure webinar marketing. I had notebooks upon notebooks of useful information and amazing ideas sitting on my desk. But what I didn't have yet was clients. I had spent all this time learning and almost no time actually doing anything. I'd felt so busy and yet I had no results to show for all my effort.

It seemed like a good time to start implementing some of the stuff I'd learned. So I got busy again. Up till all hours of the night, working every weekend, exhausted and spent, I tried every formula under the sun. Even though nothing felt natural or like "me" I pushed through because if it could generate success for the person who created it, it had to work for me too, right? I was working constantly, I was tired, and my poor husband was growing weary of going to bed alone every night while I stayed up in the living room plugging away, building my empire.

Finally, the dam broke. We'd just moved to our dream town and I wasn't finding any time to enjoy it. I was miraculously making money in my business but every dollar was hard-earned and stained with my blood, sweat, and tears. Exhausted and spent I knew there had to be a better way but I was terrified to stop. I reached out to entrepreneur friends who were doing things differently and asked what was working for them. I read books on surrender and reconnected to my Source for guidance. I built up my faith muscle and reminded myself of how strong and capable I was. And then I started following the Rituals outlined in this book. And suddenly everything changed.

I prioritized my health and wellness. I went to bed at a decent hour - regularly. My husband and I were able to enjoy our weekends together exploring the California coast. We got pregnant and our amazing daughter August was born and I was able to pull back even more. Oh, and the business stuff got easier too. Clients showed up more easily. I even had my first $40,000 week. And it felt effortless.

It doesn't have to be hard. You can create the Results That Matter to you and also have a life at the same time. You can and you **must.** And this book was written to show you exactly how to do it. If you've ever thought to yourself, *I know exactly where I want to go, but I have no idea how to get there,* my RESULTS Rituals are about to reveal everything you need to create a custom strategy to grow your business and get the results you really want. If you follow the RESULTS Rituals that lie ahead, and believe that it's possible, nothing will stop you. The strategy you're about to create for your business will feel fluid, fun, and easy to accomplish. And you'll get awesome results all while enjoying the journey to creating them. (Imagine that!)

The time is now, my friend. The world is waiting for you to show up and make your impact, and it's never going to happen while you're still wearing that Deputy Hustle badge. Oh wait, I forgot. You already set fire to that ugly piece of tin 10 paragraphs ago… GO YOU!! Now warm your hands by the bonfire and let's start this journey of yours, together. I'm with you the entire way.

# CHAPTER 1

# THE *RESULTS* RITUALS

*"Big results require big ambitions."*

*Heraclitus*

*"You can only have two things in life,*
*reasons and results. Reasons don't count."*

*Robert Anthony*

'm a big fan of efficiency. If there's an app, system, or process I can implement to make my life easier, you'd better believe I've tried it. I've even been known to choose the peril of potential death or serious injury by filling my arms with so much stuff you can barely see my face rather than having to make two trips down the stairs. So it's probably no surprise that I created an acronym for the transformational process this book is about to walk you through.

There are seven steps that await you in the pages that lie ahead. My RESULTS Rituals are the best of everything I've learned and implemented since my business began. They're filled with methodologies and philosophies and tactics that my clients and I have used to create success in our businesses without having to kick our own asses to do it. I'm going to outline them here for you to give you a taste of what's to come, but first I want to talk about why I'm so focused on RESULTS (besides it working out so perfectly as an acronym for my process!)

## RESULTS THAT MATTER

As a business strategist, my world revolves around outcomes. I can't help a coach generate a strategy unless I know what the goal is that they want to create. My GPS brain has to have a destination input into it in order for it to whir up and display the map to get there. (Yes, that's really how my brain works.) So naturally RESULTS are my wheelhouse.

Whenever a new client comes on board one of the first things I'm committed to doing is identifying the activities we need to put in place to help them earn back their investment as quickly as possible. I do this because it's fun! And it gives my clients something tangible to look forward to. But as far as I'm concerned, making money is only one small result that could be generated in your business or life. What's way more interesting, compelling, and motivating is the idea of creating what I call **Results That Matter**.

As entrepreneurs we tend to shoot for goals that associate with things like revenue, profit, client conversions, list size and the like. They're tied to metrics that are easy to track, so it makes sense that we'd use them as the results that are indicative of our success. But what's interesting about using metrics like these as the endgame, especially for entrepreneurs with big missions and even bigger hearts like you and me, is that they're simply not that significant to us in the grand scheme of things.

Sure, money is a great goal to get after in your business. But the **why** behind the money is an even better one. One of my favorite questions to ask my clients as we're deciding what their Results That Matter are is: *"What will achieving that metric allow you to do in your life?"* You set revenue goals because you have a specific vision of what you want your life to be like. There are adventures you want to have, feelings you want to experience, things you want to do in your life that you see the money as being the key to unlocking for you.

My clients set revenue goals so they can do things like visit their parents in Albania for the first time in 12 years, provide an opportunity for a dedicated partner to work less, move out of their in-laws' house, feel wanted and needed by clients, feel less guilt about doing the things they enjoy doing like gardening and cooking, and even to simply shop without restrictions. My revenue goals are tied to maintaining my ability to be home all day long with my daughter as she grows up. Understanding what's underneath the standard metric-driven goals we set creates a whole different trajectory for generating those Results. And when they're aligned with the things that matter most to us, like our values and intentions (more on that in chapter 4, Summon Your Excellence), our ability to create those results increases dramatically.

So what are the Results That Matter to you? The best way to identify those is to start at the surface with the goals and intentions you're currently working toward. If you're like most of the coaches and entrepreneurs I know, you're likely hoping this book will help you create a strategy to achieve one of those easily trackable results I mentioned above, like revenue, profit, conversions, or list size. These trackable metrics are an awesome place to start because, as I mentioned earlier, they generally lead to something bigger and more meaningful that you'd like them to help you create in your life.

If revenue or profit are your current game, what will the increased cash flow make possible for you? We'll get into identifying your values and intentions in more depth in Chapter 4 but for a moment think about the things that are most important to you in your life and how having more money will impact those things. Will it provide you the means to travel more? Spend more time with family? Care for an aging parent? Upgrade your shabby wardrobe? Give back to your favorite charities? Incorporate some much needed self-care into your life? Be specific and think about what the increase in revenue will actually provide for you once you have it. *"Let's live half the year on the east coast and the other half on the west coast so we can spend more time with our families"* is a way more compelling intention to work toward than simply, *"I want to make $15,000 per month"*, wouldn't you say?

The same is true for something like conversions or list growth. What will having a bigger list or generating more conversions actually do for you? Does it mean that your movement is growing and you're impacting more people? Will it give you the opportunity to create some passive income offerings that allow you to better leverage yourself and give you more free time to spend with your kids? Get to the bottom of **why** that Result Matters to you and you'll double your chance of achieving it before you even have to start thinking about the strategy.

Aligning to your Results That Matter, and creating a strategy to bring them to life, means that you're moving toward something powerful, magical, and resonant, as opposed to just a number.

That's what this book is all about. In the pages that follow you'll get another opportunity to identify more specifically what your Results That Matter are, and by the end, have a specific, customized strategy in place to achieve them. Oh, and if you follow my lead you'll also prove to yourself that you can do it by **creating an actual Result** before you've even finished the book. Yep, you're gonna practice what you're learning and get a Result **before** you're done reading. Sound good? Awesome, let's dive into a quick overview of the RESULTS Rituals, my signature process for creating the Results That Matter to you without having to kick your own sweet bottom to do it.

## RELEASE YOUR HUSTLE

This first RESULTS Ritual will help you identify your starting point on this journey. There's actually a specific reason why you feel compelled to work hard, and an even more specific reason why it **feels** hard too. We'll determine what your brand of hustle looks like and then, guess what? You get to release it for good.

## ESTABLISH YOUR EPIC MISSION

In this Ritual we'll explore what your Epic Mission is. Your Epic Mission is the biggest, most expansive Result you could create in your business or life. It's the movement you're creating in the world, and the reason that's bigger than **you** that gets you out of bed and serving your people every single day. With your Epic Mission clearly defined, creating a trajectory and strategy to make it come to life becomes a piece of cake.

## SUMMON YOUR EXCELLENCE

When you Summon Your Excellence you create a narrower focus for yourself and your business. But more important than that, you become the person who's already done the thing you're setting out to do. (Confused? Don't be; the chapter will reveal all soon enough.) If your Epic Mission feels at all overwhelming at first glance, don't worry. This chapter is designed to give you all the tools you'll need to ensure you can achieve it. I'll also share with you the framework I created for identifying **exactly** what you need to do in order to create those Results That Matter to you.

## UNCOVER YOUR STRATEGY

This will likely be the chapter you'll be most tempted to skip ahead to but I implore you to wait until you've laid the foundation of the initial three RESULTS Rituals first. When you Uncover Your Strategy you'll finally know exactly what tactics to put in place to help you create those Results That Matter to you. And even better, they'll be things that you find fun and easy to implement. No more hustle required to get stuff done, my friend!

## LAY DOWN YOUR COMMITMENTS

In this Results Ritual I challenge you to not only commit to your strategy for bringing your Epic Mission to life, but also to be willing to explore what your behavior says about what you're really committed to. I'll share all about one of my favorite tools for creating results, The Big Knowing, and give you the opportunity to check your integrity by understanding the power of investing in yourself. And you'll walk away with a custom-crafted Declaration Statement to carry your motivation and inspiration forward as you implement that awesome strategy you'll create.

## TAP THE MAGIC ELIXIR

I won't spoil the surprise and tell you what the Magic Elixir is yet, but suffice it to say it's something you'll be excited to tap into. In this chapter I also rip the veil off of Humanity's Biggest Lie so you can quit falling for it once and for all. I'll tell you why I completely shifted my business model midstream this year and I'll also share an automatic manifestation tool that you've already got in your toolkit but may not even realize is there. (Sweet!)

## SPRING INTO ACTION

In our final RESULTS Ritual I share how important it is to ensure you're taking the **right** actions for you, and what can happen if you don't. I also talk about why creating expectations and being impatient about outcomes can actually be a fatal flaw to generating your Results That Matter. Then I'll share a quick tactic for knowing which actions will get you traction the fastest, but be forewarned… it requires you to be ok with the idea of getting a little uncomfortable! Hey, I've got your back all the way through this book and beyond, so don't sweat it in the slightest.

Throughout the book you'll notice I've included tools and resources for you to grab outside of the book that enhance your application of everything you're learning. They live outside of the book because they were either too robust to include in these pages, or they enhanced the e-reader experience to have them available online. I know that crafting a business strategy can be tricky! And especially so when it requires you to shift out of hustle mode and adopt fun and ease instead. It may feel foreign at times, or confusing to understand. I get it. That's why these extra tools and resources are there.

I believe in the power of implementing and integrating learning as quickly as possible. This book does you no good at all if it just sits on a shelf or collects dust in your Kindle library. The real power comes from you actually using the information within these pages. Those additional tools are intended to provide the extra juice you need to ensure that you get that strategy you create in place so you can generate those Results That Matter to you and change your business and life forever. I want you to change the world!! So be sure you visit the links, download the tools, and do those exercises. They're the best gift I can give to help you get where you want to go as quickly as possible.

Alright, onward to your first RESULTS Ritual. It's time for you to say goodbye to that dear old friend of yours and Release Your Hustle once and for all!

# CHAPTER 2
# RELEASE YOUR HUSTLE

*"How we spend our days is of course how we spend our lives."*

Annie Dillard

*"I have one thing to say, you better work."*

RuPaul, "Supermodel"

W hat was your first word? Was it the standard "mama" or "dada"? If you grew up with a pet perhaps is was your pup's name, or if you're anything like my foodie daughter it might have been "yum". Mine was something a little different.

According to my mom, the story goes like this: I was somewhere in the vicinity of 12 months old, sweet and angelic with my perfectly chubby cheeks, blue eyes, and (formerly natural) light blonde hair. Playing quietly in our family room, I was lost in the sea of orange shag carpeting. Mom, in her standard bare feet, bell bottoms, and short-sleeved tie-dye, looked on adoringly from the yellow-flowered couch on the other side of the room while I attempted to fit a square peg into the round hole of my block sorting bin.

It wasn't working out.

I tried every which way to jam that square peg into that round hole. I pushed as hard as I could. I tried it from a different angle. I used the mallet that came with the toy. I was determined and committed to make it fit! But alas, as we all know, no matter how hard you try, unless you've got a belt sander or hacksaw, you just can't fit a square peg into a round hole. This made me one aggravated little cherub. I started voicing my frustrations.

At first mom wasn't sure what she was hearing. From across the room it sounded like a cute little baby chant. My first words hadn't been uttered yet so her ears were constantly perked at the ready for the monumental milestone to occur. When it seemed clear this was yet another gibberish-induced false alarm, she smiled and went back to reading her Stephen King novel.

Then it got louder. Mom put the book down. The more frustrated I got the more vocal my chant became. Mom listened more intently. Syllables started to form. Mom sat up straighter on the couch. Consonants connected to vowels more succinctly. She strained to discern if it was still the ramblings of a pre-talking infant or if she was actually bearing witness to my genius at work. Suddenly the all-familiar phrase came through loud and clear. It was something she'd heard my father say many, many times over the years. The proud moment had finally arrived! My first word was…

"Fuckendammit."

And thus my hustle was hatched. I guess some of us are just born with it, while others of us develop it over time. Maybe you grew up in a household of workaholics or Type A overachievers and that spawns your hustle. Or it's just in your DNA from birth to want to check items off a perpetual to-do list by any means possible. In truth it doesn't matter at all where it came from. You can successfully Release Your Hustle with the help of this chapter whether you know its origins or not.

## THE PROBLEM WITH HUSTLE

Dictionary.com defines "Hustle" as, "*to push or force one's way; jostle or shove.*" and "*to be aggressive, especially in business or other financial dealings.*" That sounds about right to the infant in me with her blocks. What about you? When you think about what it's felt like to hustle all this time, do the words "pushing", "forcing" and "aggressive" ring true for you? I'd be surprised if you said they didn't. When we're hustling, we're working our little asses off on everything under the sun that we can think of to help us grow our businesses. We're getting up early and going to bed late. We're missing out on all the things we love in life in the name of the goal we're going after (which often is related to finally enjoying all those things in life that we keep missing out on now; how ironic!) And much of it feels **hard**. And annoying. And burdensome.

The reason it feels hard and annoying and burdensome is the key to Releasing Your Hustle. It's because doing all of those things, following all of those formulas, **simply isn't you.** The 15-email opt-in and nurture campaign you're slogging through? It just isn't you! The video series you can't seem to get yourself to record? That ain't you either! The networking event you'd rather jab a salad fork in your eye than attend next week? You guessed it; not you. And your spirit and intuition know it so they jump in and remind you loud and clear by showing you how icky and awful it is to do those things. The resonance to who you **really** are simply isn't there, so those activities feel frustrating and exasperating to accomplish.

And what's even more obnoxious about it is that all that hustle means we're working terribly inefficiently. If the results we're getting actually do meet the metrics we'd set when we started on the road after that goal, most often it's at the cost of exhaustion and dissatisfaction. We should be overjoyed when we close the cart and achieve those two-week launch numbers we wanted but instead we're just excited to take an effing nap already. My buddy Gary Vee says, *"We are in control of the one asset that we all give the most f#%ks about, and that is time."* Amen! And if all our time is spent pushing up against resistance to get through to the other side of some task or tactic, how efficient can we possibly be?

## BUT WHICH RESISTANCE IS IT?

Resistance breaks down in two ways. There's **fear-based resistance** and there's **spirit resistance**. In short, fear-based resistance shows up when your inner committee goes on red alert, full action stations, shields up, guns loaded, threat level crimson because you've taken a teeny tiny, itty bitty step toward something that might encourage you to grow or change even just a little bit. Spirit resistance, on the other hand, happens when your spirit, gut, or intuition throws up a flare telling you that the thing you're doing **just doesn't jibe with who you really are as a person**. It's like you make a decision to do something and your internal guidance system says, "whatchoo talkin' bout, Willis?" I'll delve into both in more detail here but let's start with fear-based resistance because it's the most fun to dismantle and debunk.

Fear is a god-awful thing, isn't it? And especially so when we don't notice it's there, insidiously influencing our decisions and actions. But we're smart, capable, trained coaches, how does that happen to us, you ask? Well, we're smart, capable and trained, but we are also entrepreneurs having a **human** experience. We've got egos and inner critics running around ram shod inside our heads with us, making it nearly impossible **not** to bump up against some form of internal opposition to things that require us to grow and stretch ourselves.

Our ego is here to keep us safe and warm and cozy. It works with the fancy amygdala up in our brain to assess a threat and help us flee when necessary. Our cave-dwelling ancestors found our ego especially friendly and helpful when they'd inadvertently wander into a saber-tooth tiger den. It's the voice in our heads that says, *"Wait, you're gonna do what now? Did I just hear you say something about us changing in some way, shape, or form? That sounds like it's gonna be pretty uncomfortable. How about we just stay here on the couch and eat Cheetos and watch 'Friends' reruns on Netflix instead?"* That ego of ours likes things to stay comfortable and **the same.** It really, really, really doesn't like it when we try to change or grow. Its job is to keep us safe from the unknown, and guess what? Change and growth inherently live in the unknown. That's what they're all about! Venturing forth into places as yet undiscovered by us. That's why they're so exciting, powerful, and enticing to go after.

But man, our ego resists. It's scared of the unknown so it throws up all sorts of reasons and circumstances to get in the way of our ability to make change happen. We hear things like, *"but what if we fail?"* and *"oh, that's really hard, and it's getting annoying to try and finish it. We should probably just quit now"* and *"wait!*

*There's something even more fun to try over there! Let's do that instead! SQUIRREL!"* We think it's our intuition pointing us in the right direction but in fact it's that blasted ego of ours trying to keep us safe and small. Sure, it means well, but you know what? Last time I looked around my office there wasn't a woolly mammoth lurking behind my whiteboard waiting to eat me alive, so I think we're gonna be OK if we decide getting on stage is the next best way to grow our business.

And don't forget about that awesome inner critic that hangs out in our subconscious with our ego. She's the one that constantly reminds us how much we suck, how bad we are at what we do, and what a great idea it would be to just quit our businesses altogether so we can set off on the path to being the giant disappointments our loved ones always knew we'd be anyway. (MAN! That inner critic is mean!) With these two jokers at the helm of our businesses with us it's a wonder we ever get anything productive done at all. When our inner committee gathers and starts to drive up a whole bunch of unnecessary worry within us, our fear-based resistance goes into overdrive. We let circumstances, reasons, and shiny objects get in the way of progress and our dreams and goals shift to the wayside.

Spirit resistance, however, is different. As I mentioned before, it's linked to our internal **resonance**. The more tuned in we are with ourselves - who we are, what we value, what our intentions are - the easier it is to discern when something's a resonant match for our spirit or not. For most of us, especially those of us that are gut-decision makers and have a strong connection to our intuition, spirit resistance can be easy to discern. It shows up when we embark on something new and it simply doesn't "feel" right. You might notice it as you're thinking about a new offering, talking to a potential client, brainstorming a marketing strategy, even mulling over what to have for dinner. If you're not a gut decision-maker, this is where knowing yourself and your values and intentions comes in really handy. (More on that in Chapter 4, Summon Your Excellence.)

## FORMULA FOR DISASTER

Do you want to know what the real problem is here that's causing the resistance you're experiencing? The thing that's at the foundation of why you're working so hard and either feeling too exhausted to enjoy your results or not getting the result you wanted to begin with? It's exceptionally simple and yet so complex nearly every awesome coach I know misses it. The single biggest mistake I see hundreds of brilliant coaches make (and I'm going to assume that since you're here reading this book you're making it too) is this: they follow someone else's formula for success expecting to get the same result. Like cute little infant Amy, they're trying to fit a square block into a round hole!

Now don't get me wrong, I'm a recovering formula junkie myself. And in fact, I do believe that formulas, blueprints, roadmaps, 10-step action plans, and the like are really useful tools *for the right people in the right context.* The resource itself likely did create a 7 or 8-figure business for the person selling it to you. And there are certainly people out there who are built to follow it and find similar success. But here's the rub. YOU didn't create it. The intention behind it was personal to the person who built it. It worked for him or her under their personal conditions, guided by their personal values. Your personal conditions and your personal values aren't infused anywhere up in that formula of theirs!

Here's some irony for you. When I was first starting out, I built my business on this model: "*My clients come to me because they want the "steps" they need to grow so they can just go do them. I can see the steps. I'll give them the steps and they'll do the steps and they'll be happy and successful!*" I'd load them up with marketing plans based on proven formulas I'd learned, like webinar sales strategies, pre-sell formulas, Facebook marketing and the like, and my clients would get to work.

And then one of two things would happen: 1) They'd get completely overwhelmed by all those steps and quit before they even started, or 2) They'd follow that formula that worked for someone else and work their asses off implementing it only to end up so exhausted they couldn't enjoy the results they finally created.

I couldn't understand what was going wrong. They'd asked for the steps. I'd given them exactly what they asked for! And yet, they weren't getting what they really needed. So I scrapped that offering. People still asked for it but it simply wasn't serving them so I wouldn't offer it anymore. After lots (and lots) of research and reflection I finally realized what was missing. It all boiled down to one tiny little word. "YOU".

When you're following someone else's method for creating success, it's **their** way, not **yours**. And while it might even work for you - and for plenty of my clients it did - you likely won't enjoy the process or the results. In his killer book *Nobody Wants to Read Your Sh\*t,* Steven Pressfield, the master of resistance, wrote, "When you try too hard, you have bad ideas. When you work mechanically, you have bad ideas. When you follow formula, you have bad ideas. When you're desperate or panicky, you have bad ideas." YES! I'd go one step further and say that beyond having just bad ideas, you end up with bad results. Even when the results you end up with are the ones you thought you wanted to begin with!

## *YOU* ARE YOUR BEST STRATEGY

What if instead of following someone else's method for finding success you focused **only** on the activities that brought you joy? What if your tactics included things that were really in your zone of genius? What if your strategies were based on things that you already knew you enjoyed doing **and** had actually been proven to work for you in the past? How might you feel differently working every day if this was how you operated in your business? That's exactly what we're building here with your Hustle-Free Business, my friend.

Let's Release Your Hustle right here, right now. Ask yourself the following questions to get clear on where you are right now so you'll know what to put in place as you develop your custom growth plan throughout the rest of the book. I've got a free video training available as part of my Hustle-Free Business Toolkit that walks through the unraveling process in even more detail. If you're really committed to doing things differently to grow your business and can't wait to get started, you can download that at HustleFreeBusiness.com/toolkit right now.

Once you're done with these questions, you'll be ready to move on to Step 2, Establish Your Epic Mission. This is where things start to get really fun! What would it be like to wake up every day knowing that everything you set out to accomplish was going to lead you on a path to living your purpose? How would you be different if you went to bed every night feeling fulfilled and like you'd served the people you're here to serve? What would be possible for you if you were living, breathing, and taking action toward building the movement you're here to build in the world? If the words *it would be freaking awesome!!* are scrolling through your consciousness right now, bravo! You're on the right track and you're reading the right book. Answer the questions below to Release Your Hustle once and for all, then you'll be primed and ready to Establish Your Epic Mission.

# QUESTIONS TO ASK YOURSELF:

1. What projects, initiatives, marketing efforts, personal endeavors, am I working on right now that feel hard? And which ones feel easy and fun?

2. Where in my business and life do I notice I keep bumping up against resistance of some sort?

3. What shiny objects keep attracting my attention away?

4. How much time am I spending working right now? And how much of it feels light and fun?

5. How do I feel about the results that I'm generating right now?

6. What am I missing out on right now because I'm so busy hustling?

7. What would I rather be doing if I weren't working?

## CHAPTER 3
# ESTABLISH YOUR EPIC MISSION

*"What you can do, or dream you can, begin it.*
*Boldness has genius, power, and magic in it."*
John Anster via Johann Wolfgang von Goethe

*"Aim high, and you won't shoot your foot off."*
Phyllis Diller

E arly in 2016, I hosted my first virtual co-working call for a group of entrepreneurs I knew. The gist was we'd gather together on Zoom and everyone would get busy gettin' stuff done. My feeling was that being together, even virtually, would create a great space for productivity to happen. And since I didn't have many tasks to accomplish myself that day I decided to make myself available for brainstorming "hot seats" for anyone who needed some strategic help in their businesses. The call was a huge success and subsequently led to the forming of my awesome free community, The Growth Tribe, and a weekly tradition of free

Momentum Monday Co-working calls for any Tribe member who wanted to join.

On this first call, a friend of mine from Marie Forleo's B-School community asked for some help vetting a new business idea she had in mind. (Yes, I finally made it into the pearly gates of B-School!) Yola had been a ThetaHealing practitioner for the last 13 years, mostly using her license and skills as a side gig to supplement her income from other full-time jobs. She came to the call that day with an inkling of an idea for something new to create that was based on something she was really excited about.

All her life, Yola has loved organizing things. She regaled us with a story that her grandmother loved to tell about how at two years old, Yola couldn't enjoy playtime until all her toys were organized perfectly. And, in fact, it wasn't just the toys that she set out to organize, but her Nana's entire apartment fell into her tiny two-year old organizing clutches. A few months before the call, Yola had read Marie Kondo's *The Life-Changing Magic of Tidying Up* and KonMarie-d her home, as she puts it. The liberation she felt by following Marie Kondo's method was intense, immense, and inspiring. Yola now wanted to share that same kind of experience with others but wasn't sure if it was a) a good idea, or b) if it was indeed a good idea, how on earth she'd turn it into a viable business.

As soon as Yola started talking about her background in ThetaHealing and her passion for organizing, my GPS brain started whirring and the map began to form. I asked Yola question after question to dig deeper into what excited her most about organizing in general, but more specifically, about helping people clear out their unwanted stuff. What I learned through the course of this call was that it wasn't just that Yola was passionate about helping people color code their closets or stack their books in alphabetical and size ascending order. She was most excited about the power she could help them generate by eliminating the things in their lives that weren't serving them. As soon as Yola said that, we'd found the connection to her **Epic Mission.** Suddenly her real job was to help free people from their physical and energetic limits so they could fulfill the purpose they signed up for in this lifetime. If she could help enough people do that, she could actually change the world. (Pretty awesome, right?)

Our second RESULTS Ritual, my friend, is to decide what **your** Epic Mission is so we can create a trajectory to achieving it. By now we've got a handle on where you are right now with your hustle. You should be clear on what you're doing that feels hard, and what results you're getting (or not, as the case may be.) Now it's time to have some fun! Let's look ahead and determine where it is you want to go, but in the most epic, unlimited ways possible.

Establishing your Epic Mission requires you to think about things that don't exist yet in your life. In the present moment, they're just ideas. Where they live now is in what I call the Field of Potential. Dictionary.com defines "potential" as *"capable of being or becoming"*. All those possibilities you can imagine for yourself, for your business, for your family, for your life, for what your Epic Mission may be, they **are** capable of being or becoming. No matter how big, crazy, or overwhelming they may appear, they actually already exist right now in the Field of Potential and are just sitting there waiting for you to call them forward. The Field of Potential exists all around us and every human being on the planet has the power to tap into it. Yep, even you! And, by the way, I'm not the only one who knows this to be true. There's an entire field of science committed to exploring how all this stuff works. Ever heard of Quantum Physics or that crazy-haired dude, Albert Einstein? This was his domain, big time.

So now you may be wondering, if we all have the power to access this awesome Field of Potential, why aren't we all living large and in charge all the time? Well, there's a trick to accessing the field and making the most of it. We have to **unlimit** ourselves. Because we're entrepreneurs, spiritual beings, powerful souls having a human experience, our brains tend to want to dictate what we can conceive is possible in our lives. Like I discussed in the previous chapter, our ego and inner committee are really committed to keeping us safe and comfortable at all costs. They create limits and boundaries to what we can conceive is possible as a means to keep us from being maimed, killed, or please-God-no, disappointed! We get stuck in our version of reality and can't allow ourselves to see bigger, more exciting (aka "dangerous") possibilities.

But when we **unlimit** ourselves, and access the Potential that's waiting for us, something magical happens. Momentum kicks in. The instant we let ourselves believe that something new, different, and awesome is actually possible for us (and I mean really, truly believe it), the seas part, windows of opportunity fly open, and Brad Pitt shows up at your door with a six-carat diamond and a marriage proposal. Momentum is an amazing tool to use to generate results fast and to move you quickly along the trajectory to achieving your Epic Mission.

# MOMENTUM,
## YOUR NEW BEST FRIEND

Let's go back to Yola for a minute as an example of what this looks like. The potential I saw in her that day was enormous. My GPS brain told me she could combine her passion for organizing with her skills and talents in ThetaHealing to help people clear out the clutter in their physical spaces while simultaneously helping them install new energetic programming that would reveal the powerhouses they were deep inside them. They'd free up their physical space and their mental space and finally have room to allow themselves to create big, massive shifts in their lives. I saw dozens of ways that Yola could offer this service to people and couldn't wait to help her build the offering. I invited her to become a client in my group program so I could do just that. She couldn't wait to get started.

Yola and I dove right in developing a plan for her new offering. We strategized and got clear on who she really wanted to work with, how she'd market the program, what her pricing would look like, and what her offering would include. Her excitement was palpable, and she had total clarity about where she wanted to go. As a result, the momentum she generated those first few weeks was insane! She brought on three beta clients right away and immediately made back her investment in my program. (Wahoo!) She accessed the Field of Potential, saw what was possible in her Epic Mission, created a trajectory to achieve it, and took action that generated tons of momentum. It was inspiring and awesome to watch.

About four weeks in something interesting, yet not unexpected, happened. The initial momentum from the novelty of the potential started to wear off. This allowed Yola's old patterns of self-doubt to start creeping back in. It worked like this: Yola saw the potential for what she could create. She set out on a trajectory to create it. She started making progress toward changing her own life, along with the lives of countless clients she'd impact along the way. And BAM! Her inner committee raised the high alert and said, *wait, wait, wait... We're changing too fast here! You're getting really big and powerful and that's really scary! Plus, how can little old you possibly change the world? What if this so-called Epic Mission of yours fails? What if you end up humiliated??? We can't let that happen... Let's go watch some Gilmore Girls reruns in bed instead.* As soon as that happened, all her old, habitual programming kicked in and her results started to stagnate. The excitement that had been her fuel at the beginning was replaced with self-doubt and fear. Where before she'd been willing to take on the world, talk to anyone and everyone she thought she could help, and knew exactly how beneficial her offering was, now nothing felt solid, certain, or valuable. She was completely overwhelmed and retreated to a way of being that felt way more comfortable, familiar and safe.

Have you ever experienced this? It's OK to admit you have, you're in good company. I and every entrepreneur I've ever known, including (or maybe especially) the most successful ones, understand what this feels like. Powerful people like Facebook COO and best-selling author Sheryl Sandberg, esteemed poet Maya Angelou, actress Natalie Portman, Starbucks CEO Howard Schultz, and countless others all admit to feeling like a fraud at the things we all see in them as their brilliance. No matter how successful we are or how much potential we can generate, that humanness within us makes us all susceptible to overwhelm and self-doubt.

My genius friend and leadership coach Kelly Sheets describes potential as being like a bubble. When you set an intention and start to go after it, you generate all that awesome momentum at the beginning and your potential bubble gets bigger. But then your inner committee gets triggered and scared, which we experience as being overwhelmed, so we find any opportunity we can get to pop that potential bubble and deflate ourselves back down to a much safer, more manageable size. We see the bigness of what's possible, it scares the bejezus out of us, and we retreat into our rabbit hole where it feels comfy and cozy.

## HOW UNCOMFORTABLE CAN YOU GET?

This is exactly how it went down for Yola. When her inner committee raised the threat level to red, she started experiencing this gnawing discomfort all the time. She kept telling herself that she simply wasn't good enough to do this work, much less live out her Epic Mission. It made it nearly impossible for her to make forward progress in her business. Once I got wind of what was going on, we did some digging to uncover where that limiting belief came from. Ultimately, she just couldn't own how tremendously valuable her skills were, especially with her ThetaHealing practice. Even though she'd helped hundreds of people over the years with her work, she'd had one experience years ago that didn't work the way she'd intended. It rocked her self-confidence and gave her inner committee all the fuel it needed to feed her *but-I'm-not-good-*

*enough* fire for years to come. Her potential bubble kept shrinking back to its extra small size because she didn't fully trust herself to show up for her clients and get the results she was promising.

Here's the thing. The discomfort is real. I've experienced it, Yola's experienced it, you've experienced it. We feel it whenever we try to take action on things that will help us really grow our businesses or bring our Epic Missions into reality. Having sales conversations feels icky and strained. Writing copy to describe what we do feels unnatural and confusing. Building relationships with people who could become potential clients stirs up unexplained tummy butterflies and nausea.

What **isn't real** however is the belief underneath it. It may feel real (and good lord, I know there are times it does), but in reality that belief is just tied to some fear your ego made up a long, long time ago to keep you cozy and comfortable. And what's so awesome is that once we realize that the thing causing the discomfort isn't real, then we can actually sit with the discomfort and let it pass rather than run from it. When we do that our capacity to allow ourselves and our business to really grow elevates exponentially. Do you know those Matryoshka nesting dolls everyone brings home as a souvenir when they visit Russia? It's like we start out as the tiniest itty bitty doll in the set, and as we encounter opportunities to face our resistance, feel that healthy discomfort, and get to the other side of it, we level up to the next size Matryoshka doll. Our capacity to grow gets big and **stays** big because that ultimately becomes our new size. Letting the discomfort exist instead of retreating into our comfortable way of being is the absolute fastest way to create Results That Matter and bring your Epic Mission to life.

Yola was finally able to level up to the next size Matryoshka doll when I helped her connect to two critically important things. First, I helped her realize just how valuable the work she does truly is. Yola, like **all of us**, spent entirely too much time buying into the story she'd created that what she could do for people wasn't all that special. It came easily to her, and since she'd had that one funky client scenario years ago, she had given her inner critic all the proof it needed to define her talents as second-rate, at best. We uncovered dozens of other life-changing results she'd created for her clients, which helped her also see how unique and special her skills and process actually are. With this new understanding, Yola was able to connect back into the Field of Potential and see just how possible it actually was for her to achieve her Epic Mission. She now knew that she absolutely could change the world, one client at a time.

The second thing I helped Yola connect to was just how important her mission truly was. Allowing herself to get in her own way, to focus on her own limiting beliefs and let them deflate her potential, simply wouldn't cut it anymore. Her people were out there waiting for her to show up for them. They needed her! And she was actually doing them a terrible disservice messing around like this. Once Yola made this connection, it was like the Evil Queen's spell had been broken and big, powerful Yola was back. She snapped to attention and we jumped headfirst into creating a new plan of action for her to achieve her Epic Mission. New ideas and momentum started flowing at hyper speed, even faster than before, and she was booking more clients than ever by the end of the week.

Are you ready for the best news yet? The same principles that moved Yola forward apply to you too. No matter what your inner committee may tell you, what you're here to do is valuable. YOU are valuable. And just like Yola, you simply don't have the luxury to mess around anymore. Your people are absolutely **dying** for you to show up and be their dream come true. It's your frickin job, so quit stalling and go do it!

Full transparency here; do you think writing a book like this is easy? Uh, newsflash… No, it's not! I hit resistance all. the. time. *Who am I to help these coaches with anything? Why would anyone listen to me anyway? I should probably throw in the towel altogether because I'm a big effing fraud.* Is anything my inner committee says to me based in fact? Absolutely not. And yet I still hear it and have to remind myself moment to moment what's actually important. I know that this information is necessary to get out in the world. You need it! You can't do all the things you're here to do if I succumb to the fear of my potential. My Epic Mission is just too bloody important to me. **Your success** is just too bloody important to me. And so I push through the discomfort and persist.

Bottom line is this. You've got to know where it is you're going, and specifically what your Epic Mission looks like, in order to create a trajectory to get there. And if you want to stay on track to getting there you've got to connect to some reason bigger than yourself to fuel you on the journey. Why do you want what it is that you want? Why do you want it for you and why do you want it for the world? Your reason must be something that leads you to regularly connect to the idea that you don't have the luxury to mess around anymore. That's what happened for Yola. That's what's happening for me as I write this book for you (and has happened at every evolutionary moment in my life and business). That's what needs to happen for you too.

Now that we're fired up, let's take some action! Answer the questions below to help clarify what your Epic Mission is and why it's so important to you to achieve it. If you think you're already clear on what it is, I'd encourage you to answer the questions anyway so you can ground into them as you go through this process in the book. If it feels a little overwhelming to think about creating a plan to achieving your Epic Mission, know that's totally ok and totally normal! (It wouldn't be epic if it were something small and manageable, would it?) The next chapter will walk through the exact framework you'll use to ensure you actually can achieve it. Pretty awesome, right? Well don't jump ahead, answer these questions first to get that vision clear and then you can hop to the next step in bringing it to life.

## QUESTIONS TO ASK YOURSELF:

1. If you were standing on top of Mt Kilimanjaro and had one thing to shout to the masses that would help them understand the most important thing in the universe, what would you shout?

2. Why is that important for everyone to know?

3. Who are you here to serve? Who is just dying for you to step up and be the leader they need you to be?

4. What are they waiting for you to help them do/figure out/ solve for themselves?

5. What will happen to them if you don't pursue this Epic Mission?

6. Why do you care? Why is it so critically important that you show up and do this work?

7. Why is now the time?

8. OK, so what is your Epic Mission?

# CHAPTER 4
# SUMMON YOUR EXCELLENCE

*"Our job in this lifetime is not to shape ourselves
into some ideal we imagine we ought to be, but to find out
who we already are and become it."*

*Steven Pressfield, The War of Art*

*"When I get sad I stop being sad and be
awesome instead. True Story."*

*Barney Stinson, How I Met Your Mother*

D id you know that in Thailand, 94% of the population is
Buddhist? This means you're likely to find a Buddha artifact
or likeness pretty much everywhere you turn. In the early
1800's, the Thai king got wind that there were a whole bunch
of Buddhas hanging out in dilapidated temples throughout the
country. Well that just wouldn't do so he ordered that they all be
brought to Bangkok, the new capital city, to be properly displayed.
One 10 foot, 400-year old, plaster Buddha in particular was moved

from the ruins of a city that had been invaded and decimated by the Burmese army decades earlier. This simple, but very large, stucco Buddha sat in its new Bangkok temple for the next 150 years, but that's not the end of the story for this giant Buddha.

In the 1930's, the big Buddha was on the move again. Its original Bangkok home had fallen into disrepair, so it was relocated to another temple to spend its days. Since it was so enormous, the only place the Buddha could sit was in a makeshift shack on the temple grounds. Maybe not the nicest place for a revered deity to hang out, but it was the best they could do with such a giant statue. Our big guy stayed in that shack for twenty years until a large enough building was finally constructed that could properly hold his size.

Much care was taken in transporting our giant Buddha to his new, more appropriate home, but being so heavy and tall he was quite unwieldy. While moving him out of his old shack and into his new temple, the five-and-a-half ton colossus toppled over. Plaster and stucco shards shattered all over the floor. Fearing the revered Buddha was ruined, the moving process was immediately stopped so the situation could be assessed. Upon inspection of the ancient relic, an incredible discovery was made. The areas where the plaster and stucco had broken away revealed that beneath the modest external layers was a core of **solid gold**. No wonder he weighed so much!

Unbeknownst to almost everyone, back in the 1700's, fearing the fateful Burmese invasion, the villagers from his original home covered their beloved Golden Buddha in plaster and stucco to protect him from theft and destruction. Only they knew the true value beneath the subdued layers of his exterior. Once the city was destroyed and the Buddha moved to Bangkok, the secret of his value was lost, seemingly forever. If you can believe it, at current market value, our friend, the Golden Buddha, is worth upwards of $250 million. $250 million hidden under plaster and stucco and forgotten for hundreds of years! How crazy is that?

I share this story with you not because I'm a fan of Buddhist history or Thai culture. I'm introducing you to the tale of our buddy Buddha because it's a perfect metaphor for our next RESULTS Ritual. You've spent time Releasing Your Hustle and Establishing Your Epic Mission. Now's the time to focus in on **who you need to be and what you need to do** in order to bridge the gap between where you are now and where it is you want to go. And it all comes down to revealing that solid gold core that exists deep within you, what I call your Excellence.

## WHY WOULD I FORGET MY EXCELLENCE?

Just like the Golden Buddha, we spend most of our lives layering on a facade to keep us safe from perceived threats. Life's experiences, the relationships we encounter, and our own fears create layer after layer to disguise and dull our luster. And with each layer we pile on, our connection to our Excellence becomes more and more distant. What's heartbreaking about it is that this Excellence that lies within all of us is actually our natural way of being. It's who you were intended to be when you were born and it's often who you seek to become when you set out to improve yourself later in life. And the craziest part is that even though we think it's hard to become a "better" version of ourselves, it requires way more effort to **not** be that amazing you that already lives inside of you. You are actually working really hard every single day to **not** be that Golden Buddha.

So why do we do it? Why do we allow our real selves to be buried beneath layers of fear and self-doubt? What causes us to put on this facade and completely forget just how awesome we actually are? We simply can't help ourselves. We live a lifetime of experiences that provide countless opportunities to cover ourselves up. And then we create habits in our lives to confirm these layers need to be there.

Take a moment and think back to your earliest memories of childhood. Can you remember a time when you lived with complete abandon? Whether you can remember or not, I'm certain those experiences were there. You ran free and wild, you said the first thing that came to your mind with no fear of consequences or judgment, you laughed hard and loud all the time. You were completely, unapologetically **you**. That was you in your Excellence. Carefree, fearless, and you loved yourself without conditions.

But then someone told you that you were too loud. Or to calm down. Or that you were doing it wrong (whatever "it" might be). Someone said that you needed to be less like you so that you could conform to what made them feel more comfortable. Those were the first layers of plaster being patted on your vibrant golden Excellence. And each layer planted a seed of doubt within you that turned into habitual ways of being to confirm you needed to be toned down. Your self-talk changed from *I can do anything!* to *I'm a giant failure.* You'd catch yourself before speaking up to share your opinions because you figured it was just you being a loudmouth again. You would allow more and more and more plaster to be layered on until finally you forgot the real value that exists within you. Check in with yourself right now, for instance. How certain are you *really* that you've got what it takes to see your Epic Mission through to completion? My guess is not very.

My buddy Gary Vaynerchuk said once, "The fear of losing trumps the excitement of victory for so many people". We go through our lives letting fear of judgment, ridicule, abandonment and the like plaster over that which makes us who we are, simply so we can feel comfortable and safe and like we can manage ourselves in the world around us. It's almost completely unconscious and is ultimately what causes us to feel confused about our value, question our worth, and stall in our attempts to move our Epic Missions forward. You know those moments in your business where you stop and ask yourself, *wait, what am I doing again? Who do I think I am? Why would anyone pay me for anything?* All of that confusion and fogginess stems from these layers of fear we've so perfectly protected ourselves with. We spin our wheels, some of us for our entire lives, to "find ourselves" when in fact everything we ever needed was right there within us all along. Crazy? Yes. Infuriating? Absolutely.

The great news is that since we now know that everything we need is right here within us, all we need to do is tap into it and BAM! Everything can change. Let me guess... Now you're saying to yourself, *ok Amy, but **how** exactly do I do that?* I know it seems to be easier said than done, but let me blow your mind a little bit here. All you have to do is **decide.**

# BE THE PERSON WHO'S DONE THE THING

When I started the process of writing this book I knew that what I wanted to create was more than just a book. I wanted to start a movement. I wanted to change the way entrepreneurs worked in their businesses so they could grow, get results, **and** enjoy their lives at the same time, knowing that this would ultimately ripple out and change the world! I wanted to spread the word to as many coaches as possible that those things didn't have to be mutually exclusive. And as my Epic Mission got more and more clear, my overwhelm about **how** I would do it got more and more pronounced. I'd never led a movement before, how could I possibly do it effectively now? I reached out to my mentor, Angela, about it and the advice she gave me stunned and inspired me all at once. She said, "You've got to do it backwards. You don't lead a movement and **then** become the person who's led the movement. You need to become the person who has **already** led the movement **first**, then you'll know how to lead the movement." Wait... wha? Did you catch that? I'll reiterate it here to be sure you got it.

We all presume that in order to do or achieve whatever the thing is we're trying to do or achieve, we have to **do it** first in order to become the kind of person who **can** do it. We think of it like Malcolm Gladwell's 10,000-hours rule, or that old adage, "practice makes perfect." But this brilliant shortcut says we can do the opposite. For example, if you want to grow your business to consistently bring in $15,000/month, you think you need to learn all the things and do all the things that are required to get to $15,000/month first, and then you become someone who knows how to do that, so slowly but surely you achieve your goal. It's as if you evolve into being that kind of person over time by having done the thing. But here's the reality; you may or may not actually get to that end result, even after you put in those 10,000 hours.

If you haven't generated the inner mettle necessary to do the thing you're setting out to do **before** you do it, you probably won't have what it takes to actually see it through to the end. You've actually got to **become the person** who's made the $15,000/month consistently **first**, then you'll know what to do to create that result and you'll have the inner game in place to cross the finish line. You can then say to yourself, *OK, I'm already the person who brings in $15,000 every month. How do I show up differently to make that happen? What tactics would this version of me put into place to achieve this goal?* And a whole list of things you're probably not currently doing should populate in your consciousness to help lead you to actually make it happen. I'd bet my laptop that those things you're **not** doing also happen to be things that make you want to vomit a little bit. They're not the stuff your spirit resists doing because it simply isn't YOU. They're the things that your ego red flags as "scary as all get out!" because doing them means you're **definitely** going to grow. So even though they make you want to vomit - in fact, especially because they do - your job becomes to push through that discomfort, puke, and do the things anyway so you can finally have the result you want to have! Crazy? Again, yes. Infuriating? Abso-freaking-lutely! Don't worry, I'll get into more on this whole "vomit to get the results you want" idea in more detail in Chapter 8 so, for now, keep moving forward but keep a bucket nearby for later.

Summoning Your Excellence is the process by which you become that person who's already done the thing you wish to do. It's the "how" for generating your most powerful results. By following the steps I'll outline at the end of this chapter, you'll be able to narrow your focus and create a trajectory to achieving not only your Epic Mission but also any nearer-term goals or intentions you're setting for yourself. And by the way, that more narrow focus also helps to eliminate any overwhelm that might come up as you're going after your Epic Mission.

Here's the thing, everything, and I mean everything from business to life to relationships to **everything**, is easier and more fun when we're in our Excellence. And the reason that it's easier (besides because it's you operating from the perfect, amazing state of being that you were born into) is because Summoning Your Excellence creates instant resonance with two of your most important assets: **Your values and intentions.**

## INTEGRATE AND FILTER

As entrepreneurs we tend to compartmentalize our lives. Business goes over "here" and personal life goes over "there". Our intentions and values then follow those same "here" and "there" boundaries with very little crossover. What do you think might happen though if you had one set of intentions that encompassed both? Or one set of values that you could filter both your business and personal life through? How might things be different for you if you knew for certain exactly what the most important things in the world to you were, and that every decision you made in your business and life were filtered through the lens of those values? What kind of decisions might you make differently in your **business** if it was completely clear to you what your primary intention in **life** was?

Take me for example. I've got a set of values (freedom, fun, fulfillment, love, connection, service, and possibility) and one primary intention that guides all my decisions in life and in business (to be the best role model ever for my daughter of all the magic, amazing things that are possible in life.) When I look at my options or any actions I might take, I use THIS lens to filter my decisions. If the options aren't aligned with my values or aren't resonant with that intention, I'm simply not gonna do it. Having crystal clarity like this about what your values and intentions are is the foundation to Summoning Your Excellence.

A few years ago, my client, Ruth, came head-to-head with that business/life compartmentalization problem, and a screaming dissonance between her competing values and intentions. An incredibly talented designer with kindness and positivity flowing from her in all directions, she came to me for strategic support launching a membership program she'd been planning for at least a year. We dug into all the logistics of the launch, like timing, marketing plan, key benefits and features of the program, and Ruth got to work implementing the strategy we created.

Two weeks into the process I reviewed the launch calendar and scheduled a check-in call with her about the launch email sequence she was scheduled to be working on. When we got on the phone, instead of the happy, bubbly Ruth I was used to, I found a pile of tears and resistance on the other end of the line. Ruth was completely overwhelmed by the tasks in front of her to get this membership program off the ground. I helped her get some much-needed perspective so she could pull herself together, and once the puddle of Ruth started feeling a little more human again, I began asking questions about what was really at the bottom of her overwhelm. Now, remember how I talked in chapter 2, Release Your Hustle, about how overwhelm like this isn't uncommon when our Spirit resists tactics that simply aren't "us"? What I discovered with Ruth was that it wasn't the *tactics* that weren't resonating for her. It was actually the end result.

With a little digging I uncovered that her heart just wasn't into the idea of creating a mostly anonymous Membership program. **Connection** is one of her foundational values. Ruth is a people person! She loves to connect and to see the impact she can make on her clients real-time and in-person. A membership program removed that intimate connection for her.

What I also learned on this call was that the reason she'd been set on creating her program this way was the allure of passive income. But the reason she wanted passive income isn't what you'd expect. Unlike many entrepreneurs who set out to create a passive income product, Ruth wasn't just trying to create a money machine for the sake of having a money machine. Her motivation was attached to another of her core values; **love.**

Ruth's boyfriend had been ill over the last few months, and since he lived a four-hour drive away, it was really difficult for her to make her way there to help him when he needed her. She was working a part-time job to supplement her business income that got in the way of her freedom to visit with him as well. She saw the membership program as her ticket out of her job by generating the income she needed to quit and giving her the freedom and flexibility she wanted to work from anywhere, including his house four hours away.

Once I was clear on Ruth's values a whole new map started to form in my GPS brain about what she could do instead to achieve these goals. I asked her one of my favorite questions in the world, "if there were no limits on what you could do in your business, and money didn't matter at all, what would you want to offer right now?" I barely finished the question before Ruth shouted, "I've always wanted to start a mastermind group for soulful coaches!" It was perfect. She could host the mastermind virtually, which gave her the freedom to work from wherever she chose. It met her need for deeper, more intimate connections with her clients. And best of all, it leveraged her in such a way that she could make way more money with way fewer clients to manage. (And also way fewer sales to have to generate!) Plus we designed it in such a way that all she needed to do was sell two spots in the mastermind and she'd have the income she needed to quit her part time job. The best part of all was that simply because this offering, and the new launch plan we co-created, was completely aligned with her intentions and values, Ruth sold out all the spots for it in two weeks! That is the power of knowing your values and intentions.

Alright, it's time for you to Summon Your Excellence. Because this is such a meaty topic, and perhaps the most introspective of all, I've created a free online mini-course that walks through exactly how to do it, and get the best results possible. It was simply too much to include on paper (or e-reader!) without completely overwhelming you. In the 15-minute mini-course I walk through:

- Exactly how to define your Excellence

- A process to help you identify what triggers you not being in your Excellence now

- A framework for avoiding those triggers so you can be in your Excellence all the time

- The power of role models

- And more!

To get you started however, check out the questions below. Then visit HustleFreeBusiness.com/toolkit to get the rest dialed in.

Once you're clear on how to Summon Your Excellence, the real fun begins! Our next step is to Uncover Your Strategy, which I'm pretty sure is the chapter you've been dying to jump ahead to from the moment you started reading this book. I congratulate you for following the rules here and controlling your primal planner urges. I promise that having this foundational stuff in place first will make your killer strategy that much more effective, easy to follow, and fun to implement. Thank goodness! So go answer those questions below, take the 15-minute mini-course, and then, by all means, hop into the strategy!

# QUESTIONS TO ASK YOURSELF:

1. What are all of my intentions for my personal life?

2. What are all of my intentions for my business?

3. How can I create more resonance between the two?

4. What are my values in my personal life?

5. What are my business values?

6. How can I create more resonance between the two?

7. If I had to drill down to ONE primary intention that would inspire all further decisions I made in my life AND business, what might that be?

   - For me, for example, it's "To be the best role model ever for my daughter of all that's possible in the world." Everything I do in my life and business is filtered through that intention. What might that look like for you?

# CHAPTER 5
# UNCOVER YOUR STRATEGY

*"You have to understand your own personal DNA. Don't do things because I do them or Steve Jobs or Mark Cuban tried it. You need to know your personal brand and stay true to it"*

*Gary Vaynerchuk*

*"Begin with the end in mind."*

*Stephen Covey*

Alright, my friend, you've made it! We've reached the point in the book where you **finally** get to address that all consuming concern, *HOW do I get the results I want without having to bash my head against the wall all day long???* I've got your back, baby, I promise, so put your combat boots away permanently and read on.

I'm sure it seemed like it took a while to get here, but I promise there's a method to my madness. The reason we started with our first three chapters - Release Your Hustle, Establish Your Epic Mission, and Summon Your Excellence - was to lay a rock solid foundation for what we're going to build here. With nearly 15 years of strategy and project management experience under my belt, I can tell you with absolute certainty that if you don't know where you're going, and you don't know what your starting point is, creating an effective strategy is next to impossible.

Speaking of effective strategy, let's talk a bit about what your RESULTS strategy **won't** be. It won't be filled with all the latest social media tactics. It won't be a to-do list that's six miles long. It won't be filled with lots of new things for you to learn and implement. It won't be filled with a million and one hacks for how to add six figures to your business. And it won't be filled with all sorts of trendy bells, whistles, and formulas. Unless… Yep, there's a big old "unless" in here so let me lay it on you.

Your strategy won't be filled with any of those things **unless** they align with who YOU are and how YOU like to operate in your business and life! This right here is the linchpin to this entire book, and to you getting the Results That Matter to you. Crazy, right? Whodathunk that knowing yourself was the secret to creating a strategy that really works? It all boils down to this: YOU are your best strategy.

So now that we know what your strategy won't include, I bet you're curious about what it **will** include, right? I promise, we'll get there. But first I want to talk a little more about what it looks like when you leverage the idea that YOU are your best strategy.

## *YOU* ARE YOUR BEST STRATEGY

In the last chapter, you spent a good deal of time identifying your values and intentions for both life and business as a means to drill down to one set to use as your filter for all your choices and decisions. As you start to think about your strategy, those filters come into play BIG TIME. It's critically important to know what's most meaningful to you in your life, what you stand for, and what intention you're setting for your life in order to know if you're on track when implementing your strategy. Your values and intentions act as an authenticity barometer for you. The more authentically YOU you're able to be, the easier everything gets.

I discovered just how accurate this principle was early on in my business while supporting a client's launch. Marcy had big hopes and expectations for her launch. She'd developed a following in her public-speaking training business but hadn't achieved the big numbers she'd hoped for in her previous launches. She hired me to help with strategy support from beginning to end because of my track record with previous launches, helping one entrepreneur in particular generate $40k in two weeks on her first-ever launch. Marcy had a great product. She had market validation that her people wanted it. She had a following that was engaged. I liked what Marcy stood for and was excited to help her get her program out in the world so I agreed to support her launch.

Even though Marcy seemed to have all the elements of a successful launch plan in place, including a great strategy from me, once we got closer to launching things started to unravel quickly. She had great rapport with her email list so one of the tactics we decided to implement was an email campaign to encourage them to join her program. Marcy wrote the emails like a series of stories that unfolded sharing her journey to becoming a highly-paid public speaker. They were beautifully written. Lovely inspiring stories. But they made her appear to be something I knew that she wasn't. Her intention was to sell a program to help budding speakers make $10,000/month in their businesses consistently through speaking gigs, and yet Marcy had trouble drumming up enough money each month to pay me for the strategy support I was providing her. Since her payments to me had stopped, our contract was out of integrity, which meant that my support of her launch had to pause until she could get back on track. What this also meant was that I wasn't in a position to point out to her that by putting herself out there as something she clearly wasn't her authenticity barometer was in the toilet. Her audience clearly picked up on this dissonance and her results reflected as such. She launched and generated a quarter of the goal she'd set out to achieve simply because she didn't show up as her authentic self.

## THE TROUBLE WITH FORMULAS

Incorporating YOU into your strategy isn't just limited to being authentic in your communications. Your tactics and activities need to be resonant with who you are as well or you fall into the same opportunity for peril that Marcy did. I've seen countless entrepreneurs walk into the "formula" or "blueprint" trap. Seriously, I've walked into dozens of them myself! We see someone else killing it in their businesses and then they promise to share all their secrets in the process that led them to their success. They give up the goods and we think, *hallelujah! This person just gave me the easy button to success!* But then we start to implement this surefire success plan and BAM! Resistance strikes and we get nowhere. Or we bust our asses getting results by trying to fit the round peg that is us inside the square hole that is this formula. It was made by someone else for someone else and that is why it worked for them so effectively!

That's the difference between all those other formulas and what you're building here with my RESULTS Rituals. This strategy you're creating starts and ends with YOU at its core. Made by you, for you, with your values, intentions, and specific trajectory in mind. Round peg, round hole. Perfect fit! Since I shared a cautionary tale about what **not** to do when it comes to crafting your strategy, now I want to show you what's possible when your business actually does align with who you really are.

When Laura found me, she was stuck. As a certified holistic nutritionist and wellness coach she was just starting to build her business so she was following every formula under the sun. She came to me talking about how she wanted to build her list and get more clients, and she knew she "needed to be on Instagram and Facebook to find clients", but she just wasn't getting the results she wanted no matter how much effort she put forth. She had a lot of excitement about the potential she wanted to create in the world, but since she was new to her business she was trying everything, pouring her blood, sweat and tears into her business, and not getting much traction. Everything felt hard. All her strategies felt foreign and dissonant. Nothing felt easy or fun, especially not all the social media marketing she was doing. And her results reflected as such. She was making enough money in her business to pay the rent and take care of herself, but she wanted to really grow and make a much bigger impact. She just couldn't figure out how to make it happen since everything she was doing felt so hard already.

When we started working together, the first place we focused was on understanding why it felt so hard and annoying to do the things she set out to do. We also looked at what she might really be afraid of underneath it all to figure out what was triggering her to not Summon her Excellence all the time. We talked about her intentions and values, especially how much she loved spending time traveling with her boyfriend. She told me all about her Epic Mission to change the world by helping people reconnect with their food. She knew that when people are eating better and are more connected to their food they have more energy to focus on the things that really matter. That creates unlimited potential for the world to become a better place. I was completely inspired by Laura's commitment to serving others, and her willingness to explore what was getting in the way of her success.

What we uncovered at the beginning of our time together was amazing. Laura had learned early on that you have to "work hard to survive." She grew up watching her parents work tirelessly to scrape by and support their family. They lived in fear and stress about money and couldn't see beyond that lens. She had no role models for what else might be possible in her life, so of course, this was the pattern she'd developed for herself and her business. She'd followed formulas and had not succeeded. She'd worked harder than ever, hustling to get clients, to still only eek out a living. Everything felt hard, and she was tired!

As we started to unravel all of this history, Laura was slowly but surely able to Release her Hustle. Her commitment to her Epic

Mission grew stronger with each passing day as she spent more and more time building her belief that she actually had what it took to achieve it. Summoning her Excellence only cemented that belief further. And then we started working on her plan.

We talked about all the tactics she'd tried in the past. We looked at what had worked well for her to find clients and was also fun and easy to implement. She shared about the formulas and business "shoulds" she'd tried that felt heavy, hard, and unfulfilling, like social media marketing. We brainstormed what the person who changed the world by reconnecting people to their food would do to achieve that mission. I helped her create a trajectory for leveraging her business so she could afford to travel more with her awesome boyfriend.

We took all of these insights we'd generated and collectively crafted a strategy for Laura that felt easy and fun to implement. It focused on her taking leaps of faith at times to flex her fear muscle and show her ego that she could survive. And it rounded out with tactics and action steps that felt light and fun to accomplish; no social media required! Laura went from hustling her butt off to complete freedom and ease, even adopting a new "no pushing" mantra. And the most amazing part was that her results finally started to align with her efforts.

Like magic, as soon as she shifted away from the hustle and toward a plan that resonated with who she truly is, clients and exciting opportunities started coming out of the woodwork. Offerings she'd never considered before dropped in her lap. People called her and said, "hey, I have no idea if this is something you even do, but could I pay you to do it for me?" And all of those suggestions were for things that completely aligned with her spirit, her passion, and her soul's purpose. She even started getting TV news spots and commercial gigs! If she hadn't stopped hustling, and identified what really worked for her, there wouldn't have been any room in her life for those opportunities to show up. Laura got clear on who she was and what worked for her, then she focused her energy on being more and doing more of that. Simple as that. Amazing, right?

And guess what? These kinds of results didn't show up for Laura because she was somehow "special" or "gifted" in some way. She had the same fears and limitations we all do. Her ego and inner critic got the better of her just like yours and mine do from time to time. So knowing that, I would love for you to put a big old smile on your face right now. Because if there isn't something "magical" about Laura, that means that you, yes YOU, can generate results just like her too.

OK, my friend. The time has finally come for you to Uncover Your Strategy. Now because the exercise that follows is powerfully thought-provoking and strategic, I realized it was simply too sophisticated to walk through in the pages of this book. In fact, I tried really hard to include it. I wrote everything out here and immediately realized that it was too much to incorporate and would overwhelm you on paper (or e-paper) like this. I tried to make it more concise by cutting things out but didn't want you to miss out on any of the value the full exercise provides.

My commitment is to serve your highest good. To do so I decided that instead of cutting valuable content out, I would create a free Uncover Your Strategy Master Class as a bonus to go along with the book. This online class walks you through my process step by step in an hour long video and will help ensure you craft the best possible strategy for YOU. It gave me the freedom to include everything I wanted to be sure you had so you'll have the best experience possible in Uncovering Your Strategy. I'll encourage you to make a silent commitment right now, before embarking on the Uncover Your Strategy Master Class, that you'll continue on, finish this book and create the RESULTS you were born to create. Your people and your mission need you too much to stop now. You'll find the Strategy Master Class at HustleFreeBusiness.com/toolkit.

I've got one small request to go along with the Strategy Master Class: Please don't share the link with non-readers. If you think you know someone who would enjoy the Strategy Master Class, rather than send them the link, send them to HustleFreeBusiness. com to get a free copy of the book instead! Let's keep this special between us, K?

These next three steps in your journey cement everything you've learned so far and are the keys to ensuring this strategy is successful for you. In the chapters that follow you'll gain insight into how to set commitments that actually stick. I'll reveal what the magic elixir is that helps you generate momentum and create consistent results. And you'll master the art of taking action without having to worry about motivation and inspiration first. Just like you couldn't hit the highway without gas in your car or keys for the ignition, you won't reach your final destination in your life or business with the strategy you're about to create without the next three Rituals either. The great news is that they're fast to read and even faster to implement. After this the rest is smooth sailing, I promise!

Alright, onward to your Strategy Master Class!

HustleFreeBusiness.com/toolkit

# CHAPTER 6
# LAY DOWN YOUR COMMITMENTS

*"Most people fail, not because of lack of desire, but, because of lack of commitment."*

*Vince Lombardi*

*"Try not! Do or do not. There is no try."*

*Yoda*

H
ave you ever seen that cartoon of the two guys in separate mine shafts working their way to their fortune? One guy is working tirelessly, sweating and picking away at the mine, while the guy in the mine shaft beneath him has turned around, pick slung over his shoulder, dejected and defeated having thrown in the towel on his dream. As you look to the end of each man's tunnel you see that they were both just 3 feet from the gold that they both so desperately wanted. The guy who'd turned his back on his dream was 3 feet from achieving it, leaving the other, more committed man to stake his claim to the riches only 3 feet away.

I used to use this cartoon as a visual representation of commitment for my clients all the time but didn't learn until just a few months ago that it's based on a true story! In his genius book, *Think and Grow Rich*, Napoleon Hill tells the tale of a man who'd been mining for gold in Colorado. He struck a vein that produced and borrowed money from his family and friends to purchase the heavy-duty equipment he needed to excavate and extract the millions he knew to be under the ground. With the new equipment installed, the vein continued to provide the riches he was after. Until suddenly it didn't. The vein seemed to run out and no matter what he did, the miner couldn't tap back into it again. Dejected and defeated, like our guy in the cartoon, he sold his equipment and the land to a local junk man for whatever he could get and headed back home to his family.

The junk man, however, saw more potential in the land and was committed to exploring all the possibilities. He thought outside the box and invested in a land engineer who came out to assess the vein. The engineer determined that if the original miner had continued drilling just three more feet, he would've found the gold he so desperately sought. The junk man's little investment and big commitment paid off to the tune of millions of dollars in gold excavated from that mine.

I love how beautifully (and frustratingly) this story sheds light on all of the principles I want to share in this chapter. Once you've Uncovered Your Strategy, which you did with the help of my free online Master Class and the previous chapter, our next RESULTS Ritual is to Lay Down Your Commitments. If you've ever felt like our dejected miner before or had trouble committing yourself to something and seeing it all the way through to the end (uh, can you say every free social media challenge I've ever tried???) then sit up, pay attention and take some good notes because this chapter's about to deliver the goods.

Committing to something and seeing it through to the end comes down to four principles:

1. Belief; or as I refer to it, "The BIG Knowing"

2. Knowing what you're really committed to (and it's not usually what you think it is)

3. Understanding the power of making an investment

4. Making a Declaration Statement

In his brilliant book, *Tribes*, Seth Godin wrote, "It turns out that belief happens to be a brilliant strategy." This Ninja agrees! That gold miner in *Think and Grow Rich* had belief, but only up to a point. The junk man, however, really believed in the potential for that land and what it might hold beneath the surface, which is why he was able to think creatively about what to do to find the gold. When you're committing to the tactics within the strategy you created in the previous chapter, you're committing to seeing your Epic Mission through to its ultimate finish. And no matter how overwhelming that mission might seem to be, you've got to have junk-man style, epic-sized belief that it can be done in order to bring it to life. In fact, not only do you have to believe that the thing itself can be done, but you have to believe that YOU can be the one to do it. Yeesh, that's scary! Which is where The BIG Knowing comes in.

## THE BIG KNOWING

The BIG Knowing is a deep, all-encompassing belief. It's bigger than thinking *I know I can do it*. It's actually a physical feeling you can sense within your body, inside your bones, underneath your skin, that this thing you're setting out to do is, in fact, already done. You know on a cellular level that nothing can stop you, not even yourself. It's like knowing when you go to bed at night that when you wake up in the morning the sun will have risen. It's just a done deal, no matter what.

Have you ever experienced that kind of knowing before? Maybe with a business-related project, or when talking to a prospective client you were certain would say "yes"? Or perhaps it was when you made an investment in yourself? Growing up in New York, my best friend Becky used to say, "I can feel it in my bones, tomorrow's going to be a snow day and school's gonna be cancelled!" and 9 times out of 10, she was right. It's that kind of knowing.

There's a second element to go along with that cellular knowing that comes from a place even deeper within us. It's so deep within us, in fact, sometimes it probably feels like it's outside of us, if we even believe it's there at all. That deeper knowing comes from the support that our Source energy provides. Call it God, Spirit, The Universe, whatever. There's a current that runs through all of us that has our back at all times ensuring that everything that happens in our lives happens for us in the most perfect way possible. I'll get into our connection to Source in more detail in the next chapter so I'll leave you with this for now: When you combine the knowing within yourself that the thing is already done, with your knowing that Source has your back, your commitment becomes unbreakable. Full stop. Done. Checkmate.

## WHAT ARE YOU *REALLY* COMMITTED TO?

The second element to creating a sticky commitment is knowing what you're really committed to. You may be thinking, *uh, duh, Amy, That's easy! Obviously I'm committed to the thing I'm setting out to do.* And you know what? Some of the time, you'd be right on. But only some of the time. And I'd venture to guess that "some of the time" is probably not most of the time either.

We are entrepreneurs having a human experience, and as we learned in chapter 2, Release Your Hustle, resistance is a relentless adversary that shows up frequently, no matter how committed we may be. And in fact, it shows up **more** frequently the more committed we are simply because our inner committee knows it means there's a whole lotta growth on the other side of that commitment. The bigger the commitment you're making, the bigger the opportunity to grow.

So what else might you be committed to, if not your Epic Mission? That is a terrific question! With all that potential for resistance running around inside you, you could be committed to any number of things other than your Epic Mission. Whether you're aware of it or not, those hidden, unconscious commitments lay in wait until you lose your focus or quit paying attention and then they jump in to replace your more noble commitment, tout suite. They're almost always related to something you're afraid of, and often take the form of self-sabotage of some sort as they play out in your life. Things like ignoring emails, mixing up dates and times on your calendar, not making time to call prospects to make offers, getting "confused" about what you should do next, are all great examples of what this could look like. What's perfect about this though is how easy it makes them to identify. If you can bring awareness to your behavior and thoughts from time to time you can easily discern what you're committed to.

For example, if what you say that you're committed to is your Epic Mission, are you behaving like the person who's done the thing you're setting out to do? Are you Summoning Your Excellence regularly? Are you making choices and decisions that affirm that you know this thing is already a done deal? Or are you really unconsciously committed to something else? If you find that what you're doing isn't aligned with your Epic Mission or primary intentions, take a little time to look more deeply at those behaviors so you can uncover what you're really committed to. If instead of taking immediate action to move your mission forward you notice that you're spending time stalling, there's likely a limiting belief underneath the surface that you're more committed to than your Epic Mission right now. (BTW, anything that sounds like, "but I've got to finish <insert just about anything here> **first** before I can start taking those powerful actions" is definitely a stall tactic.) Speaking of making choices and decisions, one of the things the person who did the thing you're setting out to do likely did to achieve it was **invest in themselves.** To illustrate the next point I want to share a story from my own life about how the power of investing in yourself relates to commitment, and to the **results** you can create on the other side of that commitment and investment.

## INVEST IN YOURSELF

I'm a chronic procrastinator. Ever since I was little, from daily homework assignments to big school projects with months to prepare, I've always waited until the 11th hour to get them done. I always come through on time for the deadline, but there's something about the thrill of the last minute that gets my juices flowing and kicks my commitment into high gear. Even now, I'm committed to showing up for a Live Video in my Facebook community, The Growth Tribe, every weekday at 9:45 in the morning to share insights, tricks and strategic support. It would be really (REALLY) easy for me to make a content list in advance to have a whole slew of topics to choose from each morning, but nope! Every day I wing it and allow intuition to engage as the pressure of the clock ticking down mounts. In fact, I think my intuition is more engaged and effective when the pressure is on. I know this about myself and yet with every new business project I encounter, I continue to have hopes that *this time I'll be different!* and somehow I'll magically transform myself into a person who methodically and slowly plods her way through things.

Writing this book is a perfect example of that unfolding. As I'm typing these words, I'm a participant in an amazing 9-week program that's helping me complete this manuscript. At the beginning I thought, *oh awesome! I can spread the writing out over the nine weeks and it'll feel spacious and lovely. I'm finally gonna do something like this the **right way!*** But here it is, five days before deadline, and I'm a little less than halfway done with the manuscript.

Did reading that make you nervous for me? Did it kick up butterflies in your stomach on my behalf? Well, I thank you for caring, but let me calm your fears about my potential crash and burn failure. I am actually not worried. At all. And it's not because I know I'm an expert procrastinator. It's also not because I've got so much free time on my hands, with an infant daughter whom I care for full time, a sold out program full of clients, and a husband who I love to spend time with. (Did you pick up on all my sarcasm there?) No, the reason I'm not worried about my deadline and the workload ahead of me is because I've **invested** in myself and **decided** that the outcome was already done.

The opportunity to invest in this program came at a time when we weren't flush with cash. I saw the potential for what having my book, and maybe even more importantly working with a powerful mentor, would do for me and my business. It inspired the bejesus out of me, while simultaneously giving me that *I'm gonna puke…* feeling I talked about in chapter 4. That discomfort was painful to sit with. How would I come up with the money to invest? How would I have an uncomfortable conversation with Tom about my desire to invest in myself again when he was worried about our finances? And my old standby, what if I failed and was a giant disappointment to everyone? Yuck. Puke. Growth? Bah, who needs it!

Well, I needed it, so I sat with the discomfort as I thought about making the investment. And not only did I sit with it, I **decided** that the outcome was far too important to pass up the opportunity to create it. And by making that powerful decision, I engaged Source to show me some seemingly inconceivable ways to make the investment work. Now they were only "inconceivable" because my limited logical brain couldn't conceive of them without divine support. But once I got Source on the case, the magic started to unfold. The money appeared. The conversation with Tom was perfect and supportive; I'd had nothing to worry about. The book was already written, and since it originated in the Field of Potential, the transformation that awaited me on the other side of the experience had already happened. The moment I decided it was done, it was done. The investment was the spark for all of that to show up.

Since I know we all love a good before and after story, here are the outcomes I generated from making that investment in myself and from making that powerful decision that the outcomes were already done. Obviously since you're reading the book we can conclude that I actually **did** finish it by the deadline. Maybe at this moment in time while I sit in my office typing it's not physically done, but again, its completion was inevitable the moment I pressed submit on the payment form for this program. I made back my investment in the program (times three!) already and we're still a week away from finishing. And most importantly, **I am different**. I may still be an expert procrastinator, but I have absolutely jumped up to the next size Matryoshka doll, and in fact, probably leapt two or three sizes up in the last eight weeks.

This story was about me, but this has been the case with every single one of my clients who invested and was really, truly committed to the outcome they wanted to create. Yola made back her investment in two weeks. Laura did too within 6 weeks. Jaime 3x'd her investment with one client. Ruth 4x'd hers when she filled her program. The list goes on and on.

Now you may read all that and think, *yeah, ok Amy, but my situation is different. I've got debt, or 10 kids to take care of, or an ailing parent, or a full-time job getting in the way...* I get it, all of those circumstances do actually exist in your life. But I'm calling shenanigans right here and right now on all of that. Here's the rub about investing in yourself. All those "yeah, buts" are simply resistance. It's your inner committee sounding the alert that you should be deathly afraid of the transformation that awaits you on the other side of that investment. Seriously. As we already know, your logical mind will do everything it can to keep you safe from all those perceived threats, like bankruptcy, homelessness, putting your kids in jeopardy, losing everyone you love because you're a giant failure, etc. But in the end, none of that is true of who you are.

Your inner committee requires all this proof that you're strong enough and capable enough to do the thing you're inspired to do. But it requires **zero** proof at all that any of those awful things you fear *might* happen or *would* happen. How crazy is that? We need proof that we're valuable. We need constant reminders that we've got the goods to actually help people. We need a frontal lobotomy every time someone says "no" to an offer we make because we instantly decide that means we're not cracked up for this entrepreneur thing after all. But all those coocoo crazy outlandish fears that sit underneath the surface fueling our resistance require no proof from us to worry that they might come to pass in our lives. What on earth is up with that??? Have you ever been even remotely close to being a person who would walk the path of destruction and mayhem that your inner committee is certain you're always on? Um, how about, "not even remotely"? So remind yourself of that every time they start shouting, *wait!! Don't do it!! Remember what happened to Joan of Arc??? That is SO gonna happen to us if you set out on this path to GROW!*

Bottom line is this: if you want your people to commit to you, you have to be willing to commit to yourself. And making an investment in your growth, development, or that of your business, is the most powerful way to do that. It's nearly impossible to stay in integrity if you're asking others to believe in you, commit to the transformation you provide, and invest in your genius if you're not willing to do the same for yourself. So go find those opportunities! And don't be afraid to invest BIG. The bigger the investment, the stronger your commitment to the outcome will be, and the more powerful your **results** will be. I promise.

## YOUR DECLARATION STATEMENT

Here's where we get to have some real fun with this chapter. It's time to Lay Down Your Commitments by declaring them to the world. Now by "declaring them to the world" I'm not saying you've got to go shout your commitments from the rooftops or out yourself on Facebook to light a fire under your feet with witnesses to watch you burn. Sure, you can do that. There's power in having accountability and knowing that others are there to support your journey (more on that in the next chapter too). What I'm talking about here is a much deeper declaration. It's one that you make with **yourself**. One that you're not willing to break. It's between you and Source and it represents all of the other things this chapter has been about. That you trust yourself and Source to see this outcome through to the finish. That you know without a doubt what you're committed to and are acting on that every - single - day. And that you know you and this Epic Mission of yours are worth investing in. There is immense power within you to sustain this journey. Know that and believe it. Declare your commitment to yourself. Declare it to Source. And then lock that thing down and bring it to life.

Here's an exercise you can follow to help guide that process for you. If you prefer to put pen to paper, I've got a worksheet version of this in my Hustle-Free Business Toolkit that you can download for free here: HustleFreeBusiness.com/toolkit Creating your Declaration Statement will be critical to what's coming up in the next chapter. You're going to get a ton of insight into how to leverage it and I'll share how to maximize your momentum and results with the Entrepreneur's Magic Elixir. It might be my favorite chapter in the book so I can't wait for you to read it!

## DECLARATION STATEMENT EXERCISE:

Before you dive into this exercise, I encourage you to create some magic around yourself. Make it a sacred ritual to deepen your commitment to your Epic Mission and the people you're here to serve in this lifetime. Find a quiet place, light your favorite candle or some energy clearing incense, pull a card for inspiration, and get centered. Think of your people and why you're so effing excited about serving them. Remind yourself why your Epic Mission is so critically important to them and to the world. Take a deep breath, close your eyes and envision it already completed. Then use the following prompts to create your Declaration Statement:

- This is what I know is true and awesome about ME
- These are the things the person who has done what I'm setting out to do would do
- This is the Excellence I'm Summoning
- This is my Primary Intention
- This is what I stand for
- This is what I will do from now on to ensure success
- This is what I will NOT do from now on to ensure success
- This is WHY I MUST Summon my Excellence

## CHAPTER 7
# TAP THE MAGIC ELIXIR

*"You are the average of the five people you spend the most time with."*

*Jim Rohn*

*"For the strength of the pack is the wolf, and the strength of the wolf is the pack."*

*Rudyard Kipling*

D id you know that since the day you were born, you've been living a giant lie? Your parents, teachers, friends, relatives, strangers, mass media, basically everyone you've ever known has led you to believe an enormous untruth for the entirety of your life. Don't feel too bad about it. I believed it too, as do the majority of human beings. It's a tough lie **not** to believe, especially because it was created in an attempt to keep us all safe and comfortable. It's Humanity's Biggest Lie, but I'm going to expose it, right here, right now. The ruse that's plagued our entire species for as long as we've walked the earth is this: **we are always alone.**

I know you look in the mirror and what you see reflected back appears to be a singular individual in physical form, standing there all alone. You look at your hands and legs and think, *but these are mine, and it's just me in here inside this body...* And there are plenty of times throughout the course of your life where you've felt lonely, sad, and detached from others. All of this simply validates Humanity's Biggest Lie for you. Of course you're alone! You're proving it to yourself on the physical plane all day every day.

But the reality is that the physical is only one fraction of what we're experiencing in this lifetime. I know this isn't news to you. If you've picked up this book you're hip to the idea that there's more to this world than just what we can see. But even those of us who are hip to that knowledge lose sight of it from time to time. Our awesome inner committees help us to forget, as does society in general. We travel through our lives in these individual physical bodies and can't see the energetic tethers between us so we either forget or don't believe that they're there. The irony of Humanity's Biggest Lie is that it was designed in an effort to keep us safe but in fact it just separates us, leaving us with a never ending supply of opportunities to feel lonely, alone, and sad.

This creates the most amazing opportunity for our relationship with our inner committee to grow stronger. Our ego and inner critic are in there with us all the time, after all. They keep us company, constantly reminding us just how alone and separate we are. They tell us that no one "gets" us. That we're not worthy of love. And that we'd better protect ourselves from inevitable disappointments because we, without a doubt, can't count on anyone other than ourselves.

It's like our inner committee, and the rest of the world for that matter, are on some sick, cosmic payroll, employed to ensure

Humanity's Biggest Lie maintains its hold on us in perpetuity. But deep down, all the way at the core of your being, I know you know it's not true. You're never alone. You're always connected to Source. And we're always connected to one another. The Magic Elixir we need to tap into for our RESULTS revolution to really take flight is **connection.** And that's what this chapter is all about; connecting to Source and connecting to the people you need in order to bring about the Results That Matter to you.

## SOURCE AND THAT BIG OLD LIE

So how is it that Humanity's Biggest Lie has become so powerful? It's seemingly withstood the test of time, hanging in there with us since we could walk upright and string logical thoughts together. Here's why: Its power emanates from the idea that believing otherwise makes us feel vulnerable. When it's just you against the world you can predict outcomes. You can control and manipulate how things will turn out. You can take action and feel with a high level of confidence that you've thought through all the details and your result will likely show up. There's no one else to rely on who might run the risk of disappointing you. That feels comfortable and familiar to you so you like that WAY better than the alternative.

But what if you conceded to the idea that you were not actually alone? And that not only are you not alone, but there's an energetic current running through you that helps you create outcomes whether you're aware of it or not? And that same current connects you to all the people, tools, and resources you need to succeed? Holy wow, do you know what THAT means? It means that **you're not in control anymore.** (If you could see me as I'm typing this, you'd see my BIG-eyed face right now.)

We like to be in control. We like to know what's coming down the pike for us so we can prepare ourselves to react. It makes us feel all warm and fuzzy inside if we think we've got things all buttoned up. If we throw Source into the mix, things go completely wonky. Suddenly we're not in control. We can't predict what might happen and have to find a way to roll with what shows up. But if it's not in line with our expectations, our plans go all to hell and we end up confused and lost.

What's beautiful about this, however uncomfortable it may feel to begin with, is that whether you want to acknowledge it or not, Source is always working for you. Everything you see in front of you, everything in your life to this point was created by you with the help of Source. Like a genie in a bottle, you wished for it and Source provided. Even your hustle. And especially your results.

You might be thinking, *Yeah, I get all that. I watched The Secret. I've read about the Law of Attraction. But why would I wish for inconsistent, hard-won results?* Because, Source is going to deliver whatever it is you're most committed to, whether you're aware of it or not. You might say you *want consistent results* or that you *wish you didn't have to work so hard*, but here's what you're really asking for: to continue **wanting** and **wishing** for those things to be true. Source is the most consistent partner you'll ever have in business or in life. And if **wanting** or **wishing** for something to be different is what you're focused on, then Source will deliver endless opportunities for you to continue **wanting** and **wishing**.

As I talked about in chapter 4, Summon Your Excellence, the secret here is to create awareness around your thoughts and feelings to nip that "wanting" in the bud. And, really, the fastest way to do that is to simply be the person who's already done the thing you're "wanting" or "wishing" to do. When you're being that person, there's no more wanting or wishing involved. You simply ARE that. You are someone who creates consistent results. You are someone who loves what she does and who works with ease, grace and fun to create those results. Source connects to those intentions and suddenly, like the late Dr. Wayne Dyer so eloquently put it, because "...you change the way you look at things, the things you look at change." Your perception alters, your reality shifts, and BOOM! That proof your little logical brain loves so much starts to appear before your eyes. And often it shows up right when you need it most. But the trick is to notice and acknowledge it's there! Here are a couple of examples of how that played out for me and for a client of mine.

## THE MAGIC LEAF

I went on a walk the other day to dictate my thoughts about what details to include in this chapter. As I was talking about Source, and this part in particular about paying attention to the results and acknowledging them, I noticed something out of the corner of my eye. About a foot away from me to my right, in my neighbor's yard, was a leaf floating in mid-air. No, wait. It wasn't floating. It was suspended in mid-air. It moved back and forth with the gentle breeze but didn't travel anywhere. It was tethered to that spot right in front of me, magically. I actually stopped what I was doing, quit dictating my notes and took a 60-second video of the experience.

(If you'd like to see my magic leaf, you can watch it by visiting: HustleFreeBusiness.com/toolkit)

Now, so it can continue to confirm Humanity's Biggest Lie for me, my logical brain really wanted to jump in to say, *oh Amy, you're so cute and naive. That's not magic, it's attached to a spider web, obviously.* But in reality I couldn't **see** any spider web. The magical being in me who knows what's actually true at the essence of everything knows it was a confirmation of my connection to Source. I gently told my logical brain that Source is always here and that reminders like this show up at the perfect time, **if we're willing to see them**. In that moment, I experienced something profound. And it was clear to me that it was intended for you too, which is why I felt compelled to share it here. And in fact, that experience shifted the direction of this chapter completely. But if I hadn't been paying attention, or had let my inner committee have its way, I'm not sure where this chapter might have ended up.

It breaks my heart the way most of us tend to let our inner committees do that to us. We logic away the magic because it makes us uncomfortable. As my wise, handsome husband pointed out, magic is the term we use to describe things we can't explain, and has been for hundreds of years. Things we can't understand scare us. Remember the Salem Witch Trials? That's a whole buncha crazy nonsense in response to fear of unexplainable stuff. When we can't easily label something or understand its makeup, like this leaf suspended in mid-air, it makes us nervous and uncomfortable. It messes with the comfort of things being logical, manageable, and controllable. But simply acknowledging that the magic of Source exists infuses you with power and gives you the opportunity to tap into everything it has to offer.

# REGRETFUL ABUNDANCE

So we know that Source always has our back, manifesting the most perfect outcomes for us right? But here's the painful truth about that: those outcomes are still perfect even when it feels like they really suck. This is what happened for my client, Jill recently when a client of hers tried to back out of her six-month contract in their second month working together.

Jill's client loved working with her. She'd been getting terrific results from their time together when all of a sudden, she emailed to say she couldn't afford to pay Jill anymore and would have to end their contract early. Jill felt like she'd been punched in the gut. That was recurring revenue she was counting on that suddenly dematerialized without warning. She called me in a fury of fear and anger to fill me in on the details.

When we got on the phone, Jill was ensnared in the victim trap. She said things like, "Why would she do this to me? How dare she show up to our sessions this week and let me work on her knowing she wasn't intending to pay her invoice? You know what? It's fine, I didn't want to work with her anymore anyway." Jill was pissed! And at the same time she couldn't see beyond that anger to what might be beautiful and perfect about the situation unfolding like it did.

I talked Jill through a bunch of questions to help her uncover the perfection in this contract unraveling. We determined that even though she stomped her feet and said she didn't really want to work with this client anymore anyway, that wasn't necessarily true. What didn't resonate for Jill with this client was a lack of commitment on Diana's part to be an equal participant in their coaching relationship. Diana wanted Jill to save her. Jill needed her clients to be 100% responsible for their own transformation. This clarity was brand new and a complete game-changer for her. It gave Jill a giant sense of empowerment and freedom that allowed her to step out of victim mode and look at Diana with a new sense of grace and compassion. If this client couldn't afford to pay for her support, it wasn't going to break Jill. It meant that Diana leaving would create space for someone more committed to their own transformation to show up in her place. And Jill felt an overwhelming sense of gratitude for Diana giving her the opportunity to see just how important that shift in responsibility was for her client relationships.

The amazing outcome in Jill's story is NOT that she found a new client right away. In fact, because she's such a powerful manifestor it's even more amazing than that. By making the connection to what she needed her clients to be, she actually gave THIS client the room to become that herself. Within two days, Jill called to say "I got a message from Paypal this morning that Diana had paid! Can you believe that? Now I feel like a total jerk for reacting the way I did." To which I replied, "Be careful with those intentions! Source might play along better with you in the long run if you felt something other than regret when lots of money shows up unexpectedly…" Jill got the point.

We can either choose to appreciate and utilize this connection to Source so that it works for us, or we can pretend it isn't there and **it will still work for us either way**. If it's going to work either way, why not put it to work on manifesting amazing, awesome things for you instead of more wanting and wishing? Be willing to release control. Be willing to pay attention. Be willing to accept that things your logical mind tells you are crazy maybe just aren't.

Be willing to find the perfection in the things that feel unfair and no fun. Because when you do, you give Source all the room it needs to let the magic show up for you.

## CONNECTION TO OTHERS

If you thought Humanity's Biggest Lie was a whopper, I've got another killer truth to share with you. Whether you realize it or not, right now you are employing your ego and inner critic to act as the Board of Directors in your businesses. Yep, you hired them to do this job right from day one. And man they are the absolute worst! They treat you like you're an idiot, make you constantly think you're running your business into the ground, and they say terrible, awful things to you all the time. (Especially when you're trying to get to sleep at 3 AM after a long day at work...) You start off on a new strategy to bring your Epic Mission to life and they say things like, "Oh, you'll never be able to pull that off." And, "Listen, if every bit of it isn't perfect you DEFINITELY can't launch it yet." And, "Be authentically yourself? Are you kidding me? You might as well just jump in front of a train!"

We know they mean well. I've got my own inner committee acting in that capacity in my business from time to time too. I don't know about you, but I wouldn't keep someone on staff to run my business with me who talks to me the way my inner critic and ego do, but guess what? We do it anyway, and it's nearly impossible to fire them!

As we know full well from reading Chapter 2, letting our inner committee run the show with us creates all sorts of limitations on the impact we can make in the world and the results we'll achieve through our businesses and lives. We tamp ourselves down, dull our brightness, and diminish our capacity to be seen, share ourselves, and really reach people in the way they need to be reached. But it doesn't have to be this way.

Imagine what you could do if you never worried about being rejected. What would you create if there was no voice in your head saying, *hmmm… are you sure about that?* How would you show up differently to serve and love your clients, your family, the WORLD, if nothing held you back anymore? What would it be like to just BE YOURSELF all the time? (Feel free to take a moment and sigh out loud at the relief you'd feel.) Man! The potential is EPIC. And the possibilities are endless. But first you've got to exorcise those demons of yours, and the best way I know how to do that is to replace them with some folks who see and love all the epic potential within you.

The late, great Jim Rohn once said, "you are the average of the five people you spend the most time with." Well if two of those five are your inner critic and ego, what do you think that might do to your average? As you may know, the reason our inner critic and ego are given the space and opportunity to rise in the ranks of our businesses with us and become so influential in our day-to-day is because they're typically our go-to consultants for everything. When we get a new idea, we vet it through them. When we're considering a new strategy, they create it with us. When we're thinking about what else might be possible for us, we can only see as far as their lens will let us. And nine times out of ten we don't even realize we're engaging them. We buy into Humanity's Biggest Lie, think we're in this all alone and say *I don't need any help from anybody! I've totally got this all by myself.* Which yields us mediocre results or exhaustion, at best.

But if we had a different advisory board in our corner, one who knew exactly how awesome we are and reminded us whenever we forgot, our inner committee would get demoted straight to the mailroom, stat. Community does that for us. The right people are a mirror for our Excellence. They see us as the best possible version of ourselves and hold us to that standard so we can become more of it. They give us opportunities to show up and be seen, to be vulnerable, to be authentically ourselves without fear of judgment or ridicule. They see our big picture and detect our blind spots for us in a way that we never could for ourselves since we're too close to it. And we must surround ourselves with as many of these people as we can, as often as we can, if we're going to successfully demote that nasty old Board of Directors we've currently got.

It's not just about surrounding yourself with the right people either. In order for this part of the elixir to really engage its magic, there's an active commitment that needs to take place. The right people will support your growth (and you theirs) not by letting you orbit one another in the same stationary place. The highest service you can bring to one another is to challenge each other to **grow together**. When one person says, "Hey, I'm gonna get bigger and more amazing. Wanna come with me?" and the rest of the group goes along for the ride, the mutual commitment to that growth is POWERFUL. Momentum is created and acted upon for everyone. The collective decision is made that, "When you win, I set out to win too." The community becomes a sacred container within which life-altering habit change may occur.

I watched this play out beautifully in my free online community for entrepreneurs, The Growth Tribe, earlier this year. My buddy Kelly Sheets and I co-hosted a 5-Day Fun, Ease, and Results

Challenge for my Tribe members to help them eliminate hustle and create better results while having fun at the same time. The community banded together and generated an outrageous amount of momentum. People were getting results like crazy, making money, shifting old ways of being, one Tribe member even booked two new clients in the day **before** the Challenge began simply because he'd committed to participating. The Tribe became that sacred container for this momentum to show up, and everyone who played along got swept up in its goodness. That momentum was able to flourish all week long because each Tribe member was committed to a result for themselves and simultaneously committed to supporting everyone else achieve theirs at the same time.

This is why my business model completely shifted at the beginning of this year. I went from a strictly one-to-one model to a group model overnight because of how critically important I knew this kind of support would be to my clients. I recalled the times when I had my biggest successes in my business, and realized that each success coincided with me connecting with and leveraging a powerful community of entrepreneurs. Through The Growth Tribe I continued to see over and over and over again the power community played in the results the entrepreneurs I knew could achieve. There just is no way around it for any of us, whether we're entrepreneurs or not. As human beings we simply need other people to see and acknowledge our greatness in order for us to achieve it.

## QUESTIONS TO ASK YOURSELF:

At this point you're likely taking stock of your current average of five. (I know that's what I did the moment I first heard that Jim Rohn quote!) This is a terrific place to start. Below are some questions you can use to guide that process. If you're hearing your ego or inner critic throughout your day, it's probably time to tear yourself away from that laptop of yours, change out of those comfy yoga pants and get yourself in front of some other awesome entrepreneurs like you. Extra credit if you can do it regularly and/or in-person. Then watch how your business grows, expands, and flourishes with a new board of directors behind you.

Speaking of "taking action", if you can believe it, the next chapter is our last RESULTS Ritual; Spring Into Action. Remember how I mentioned we'd talk more about doing things that make you want to vomit? Well it's time to go grab that bucket of yours. Don't worry, I'll hold your hair for you.

- Who are the people you're spending the most time with?
- Do they constantly lift you up or are they bringing down your average?
- How are they acknowledging the Excellence within you?
- Are they propelling you forward or helping you stay right where you are?
- In what ways do they challenge you to Summon Your Excellence day in and day out?
- What do you learn either directly from them or from having their influence or energy in your life?
- What actions have they inspired you to take that have help you grow and transform?

# CHAPTER 8
# SPRING INTO ACTION

*"Someone's sitting in the shade today because
someone planted a tree a long time ago."*
Warren Buffett

*"Scary is the eve of awesome."*
Laura Husson

**M**y soul sister and biz best buddy Kelly called me one day over the summer teeming with excitement. She'd been away on a camping trip for a long weekend and when she'd returned her first vegetable garden seeds had finally sprouted. Kelly was beside herself with joy about those little seedlings finally showing up. Weeks before, she'd painstakingly planted them. She'd learned all sorts of awesome methods for cultivating them. She'd tended to them like a mother hen would her precious eggs. And every day she'd look in on them and wonder, *is today the day you're going to grow, little seeds?* To finally see signs of life on this side of the dirt felt like an Olympic Gold-sized victory for Kelly.

I was thrilled for my friend! (And hoped she'd bring me some radishes on her next trip down to California from Oregon, but I digress...) While she engaged me with all the details of how her little seedlings were doing, something interesting occurred to me. Kelly's vegetable garden was an awesome metaphor for business. Every time we take an action, we're planting a seed. When we go to an event, we're planting seeds. When we spend time adding value for potential clients, we're planting seeds. When we create an opt-in sequence and email nurture campaign we're planting seeds. And just like when you're growing a vegetable garden, some of those seeds will sprout and some of them won't. What ultimately determines how both our veggie and business seeds grow and thrive is two things; planting the right seeds for us at the right time, and how we care for and cultivate them once they're planted. I guess since we're talking so much about seeds it's fitting that this chapter is called Spring Into Action, but I promise I didn't plan it that way!

## PLANT THE RIGHT SEEDS

When Kelly planned her garden and picked out her seeds she knew exactly what she wanted to grow. She's not a big fan of okra so she didn't plant any okra seeds. But she absolutely LOVES lacinato kale and fresh carrots straight from the ground, so she planted as many of those seeds as she could get her hands on. She knew what worked for her, what she would enjoy eating once they grew, and followed her intuition and personal tastes as she decided what to plant.

The actions you take in your business can follow the same philosophy. If the idea of sending out an email marketing campaign makes you want to stick a hot poker in your eye, that's probably not the kind of seed you want to plant. But if you know for certain that building relationships on social media is something you absolutely love, like Kelly did with her kale and carrot seeds, get on the old Facebook and start talking to as many of your people as you can find. This is the obvious part of the equation. But what you might not realize is that the more **resonant** your activities are with who you are and what you stand for (i.e. your values and intentions from our Summon Your Excellence chapter), the better the results you'll get in the long run. Oh, and the converse is generally true as well. Diving into those activities that are less appealing than a flaming poker in your optic nerve will create two opportunities for you: a terrible, hard, exhausting experience, and/or terrible results to match.

## NURTURE YOUR SEEDS AND WATCH THEM GROW

Cultivating those seeds of yours is the next critical element here. You can plant seeds all the livelong day but if you don't care for them properly they're just not gonna grow. Just like plants flourish in a loving, kind environment, and wilt under harsh, demanding or neglectful conditions, so do the actions we take in our business. Let's get back to Kelly's little seedlings for a second. What was interesting about her garden was when and how her seeds finally sprouted. Kelly had planted the seeds in early June and diligently visited with them each and every day, sometimes multiple times a day, asking them when they might sprout. At times she even got frustrated with her seeds, saying things like, "c'mon seeds! Grow, wouldja?!" It was almost like she was yelling at the seeds to hurry up and grow on her timetable.

At the core of everything, Kelly still loved her seeds very much but the excitement and anticipation she had about them turning into vegetables was almost too much for her to bear. It wasn't until she went away for the weekend, and left the seeds alone for three days, that they finally decided to sprout. Without the pressure or expectations Kelly had been putting on them (consciously or unconsciously) they had the room they needed to do their thing. Had Kelly not left for the weekend and instead continued her daily expectation and demand parade, I wonder what would have become of her seeds?

How many times have you found yourself yelling at your own business seeds to hurry up and grow already? It can be super frustrating to feel like you're taking action left and right but the results aren't showing up fast enough. You're dedicated to your craft, you're excited to serve your people, and you're ready to generate those results you want! It's no wonder your patience runs thin when all that action doesn't yield what you want in the timeframe within which you want it. But here's the thing… Having that demand, that the actions you take create the result you want on **your terms**, leaves no room for Source to do what it needs to do to support your journey. When you attach yourself to the outcome of "this action right here **must** lead to the result I want!" all the other limitless possibilities that exist in that Field of Potential of yours are completely killed off. You've got to let go of the demand, release any attachment to the outcome, and let the Big Knowing show up in its place to give those seeds of yours a fighting chance.

Let's compare this scenario to the actions you take in your business. Say, for example, a result you're trying to create is to bring five clients into your new program that launches in three weeks. One of the tactics you're going to use to find those new clients is to attend a bunch of networking events, which you really enjoy doing. Before each event you set an intention for yourself that you're going to meet one new client who will say yes to your program while you're at the event. You psych yourself up, practice your elevator pitch, throw on your favorite confidence-inducing outfit and off to the event you go. You've set an expectation, and are energetically demanding an outcome from attending that event; "One new client or bust!"

You arrive and take stock of the room. *Who's it going to be?* you think to yourself. Every conversation you have is laced with that intention at its core so you spend the entire evening searching for opportunities and listening for the keywords you need to hear to know you've got an opening to make an offer. You've got nervous knots in your stomach all night and get tongue-tied when people ask you to tell them what you do. Then, by the end of the event, once you haven't booked a client (which in this scenario wouldn't be a surprising outcome), you probably end up disappointed and frustrated. Over time, your memory of your experience at the event gets tainted and labeled as "just another unsuccessful activity." As far as you're concerned, this seed has become a dud and will never have an opportunity to sprout.

What if instead you went into the event with an intention of being curious about what might happen? Instead of demanding a specific outcome, you were open to any and all possibilities showing up. I guarantee things would go down completely differently. You'd attend the event feeling curious. You'd walk around talking to everyone your intuition told you to wander over to. The conversations would be fluid and organic with no preconceived agenda baked into the mix. You could float through the evening relaxed and confident because your only intention is to be there and be curious. Since you'd be really listening to each person you met you'd likely find opportunities to connect them to the people, tools, and resources they need, which might even include you! You'd likely meet some really terrific people, and might even invite someone into your program right then and there. Without the pressure of the demand that a client MUST be found at this event, your seed is free to grow at its own pace instead of yours. Plus, the openness of curiosity allows for this event to become an opportunity to broadcast dozens of seeds that could sprout at any point down the road! Even if you walked out without booking a client, the one "event seed" turned into dozens of additional seeds that you can continue to cultivate with love and curiosity over time.

Can you see, and even feel, the difference there? The trick is to incorporate The Big Knowing. If you're comfortable with the idea that some actions you take will yield results you can see and appreciate immediately, and some may either take longer or not result in anything at all, the pressure comes off and your little seeds can grow at their own pace. Just be Fonzie with your seeds. Stay cool and know that if you're taking the right actions that are aligned with who you are that the right results will show up exactly when they're supposed to.

One other really awesome thing about being cool with your seeds is that in the end, even the ones that you might label as having been "duds" or not resulting in anything likely **did** create a result for you in some other way you haven't even realized yet. For example, until very recently I've been telling the story that when I hired my first business coach I invested upwards of $30,000 and created a $60 revenue return that year. Now to be clear, that's "sixty dollars" not $60,000. I think it's kind of funny and endearing so I'm not faulting my coach in any way for that being my result. In fact, I always follow the story up by sharing all the other amazing mindset benefits I got out of working with her. But I felt clear that by making this investment I planted this seed and while it wasn't exactly a dud, the lacinato kale I thought I was going to get, in the end turned out to be okra.

I shared this story with my mentor last week and she asked me to rethink what my ROI really was on that hefty investment. Without blinking I realized that even though the tactics this coach had given to me didn't work for me while we were working together, I was introduced to a whole slew of people and opportunities that turned into revenue for me once our coaching relationship was over. In fact, I'd conveniently forgotten that this coach herself became a client of mine and invested in me almost exactly what I'd invested in her 18 months before! The seed I'd thought was a dud actually turned out to generate a 4x return on my investment in the end; I just hadn't been able to see it until that moment. Kale yeah! (Lacinato kale, that is.)

## TAKE ACTION CLOSER TO THE RESULT

Let's step back to planting the right seeds, or picking the right actions to take for a minute. As I mentioned earlier, if you want to create the Results That Matter to you, and not have to bash your head against the wall to create them, your actions need to be resonant with your intentions and values. But if you want to generate those results even faster, focus on taking actions that are **closer to the goal**. What does that mean? I like to think about it like Six Degrees of Kevin Bacon. You know, that funny game where you name any actor and then without fail can connect six actors or fewer who've worked with one another that ultimately lead back to Kevin Bacon. Like my favorite actor Matthew McConaughey for example. He was in Interstellar with John Lithgow, who was in Footloose with Kevin Bacon. That's two degrees of Kevin Bacon for good ol' Matthew. It's based on the theory of the Six Degrees of Separation, which claims that every person on the planet is somehow interconnected to everyone else on the planet within six degrees of one another.

What this looks like in your business is this: taking action that's fewer degrees of separation away from the result you're trying to create. Let's go back to our example from earlier about finding five clients for your new high-end program that launches in three weeks. Say you decide that one activity you're going to do to try and create that result is to write a guest blog post for The Huffington Post. How many degrees of separation away from the result of "five clients in my program that launches in three weeks" do you think guest blogging for HuffPo might be? Let's break it down. We'll assume that you've already got a relationship with them as a blogger so we'll skip any steps necessary to getting them to actually publish you.

1.  First you write the article and submit it

2.  Since we know that HuffPo won't want you planting an overt offer within the article, the goal of the post will be to

drive people to your website or landing page so they can be added to your list

3. They get on your list and end up in your opt-in or nurture sequence (which hopefully you've already created, otherwise we'll add a whole slew of new steps in here to get that accomplished) which will take - the experts say - a minimum of seven "touches" to get them convinced that you're a person worth considering doing business with. How long might those seven touches take? Probably in the vicinity of two weeks if you don't want to be "that girl" who vomits all over their inbox as soon as you meet them.

4. Since it's a high-end offering (think over $2,000) you're not likely to just send them directly to a sales page once the nurture sequence has done its job. You'll offer them an opportunity to get on the phone with you to see if you're a good fit to work together. Your open rates and engagement track record will determine how many of those calls actually get booked.

5. With just one week to go, now you can have those conversations, make some offers and close some clients. And hopefully the article drove enough leads to your sequence to generate enough sales call appointments to achieve your average close rate and yield you the five clients you were looking for!

OK, so that's five degrees of separation away from the result. How did that process feel as it unfolded? Was it spacious and light? Or did it feel a little overwhelming and rushed? What if you could cut that process down to two degrees instead? Let's try this and see what happens:

1.  Make a list of everyone you can think of that would be an awesome fit for this program

2.  Call them and make them an offer

Does that feel a little bit different? The further away from the result you are with the activities you engage in, the harder and more painstaking the process will be. Every. Single. Time. Now, I'm not saying that there isn't a time or place for guest blogging or email campaigns, or that your one and only tactic should always be to just make a list of people and call them up (although that's usually a pretty easy place to start!) What I'm suggesting is that you critically think about the actions you take before putting them on your ever-growing to-do list. How close can you actually get to the outcome you want to create with those actions you're taking? My recommendation is that you take action no more than two to three steps away tops. So if your goal is client conversion in a hurry, make the list and start dialing. But if your goal is to build your list so you'll have a large enough platform to entice a big joint venture partner to agree to promote your next launch, go HuffPo all the way. Bottom line, the closer you can get to the outcome, the easier and faster the result will show up.

## GO AHEAD AND VOMIT

I referenced doing the scary thing that makes you want to vomit in chapter 4 and promised to revisit it here, so I'll start off with a client story. Vannesa was stuck. Her intuitive coaching business was stalled and the course she'd built on how to create your own angel cards for your business wasn't getting any traction at all. She, like most of my clients, felt like she was working really hard but just not getting anywhere so she asked for my help in generating a plan to help her find some more clients.

After some digging I uncovered that Vannesa was taking action in her business, but everything she was focusing energy on was really safe and comfortable to complete. She had some methods for generating business that were working up to a point but they never challenged her to grow at all and certainly didn't give her any kind of breakthrough results in her business. I asked her what tactic would make her the most uncomfortable to try to find clients and she said, "recording videos about what I do and sharing them on Facebook would definitely make me want to vomit".

That kind of exposure scared the life out of Vannesa because it required her to actually be seen owning her genius. Can you relate to that feeling at all? I know I could. And so, being the sneaky Ninja I am, I challenged her to do just that. At first she tried to backpedal, but when I reminded Vannesa that the biggest transformation is always on the other side of the big scary thing, she agreed to give it a try. Within days of trying out this new, scary tactic, not only did Vannesa NOT puke but she actually booked a new client right away! And this kind of result is not uncommon at all. During our 5-day Fun, Ease and Results Challenge earlier this year, by day three (when Kelly and I introduced the "scary activity") multiple participants reported new clients, new connections, and money showing up left and right.

The point of this story is to illustrate again just how powerful it is to take action that requires you to grow. When there's a big transformation waiting for you on the other side of the activity, like showing up in your genius when you'd rather just stay small and safe, the results show up and they show up fast. Check your activities against your good old resistance meter. Anything that feels safe and comfortable can probably go to the bottom of your to-do list. And anything that feels like you'd be happier whacking your big toe with a sledgehammer than doing it is probably your spirit resisting it and should get removed from the list altogether. But all those other activities that make you want to puke, the ones that make you feel nervous and excited all at the same time, those are the ones to do immediately. They'll get you traction the fastest and will create the opportunity for you to work way more efficiently to create those Results That Matter to you.

It's important to note here that simply because you have a strategy in place doesn't mean it has to take forever to see results. We tend to think that it takes a long time to see a result because of all the steps involved in our plan. We think, *I have to do all of these things first, then a result will show up.* and we'll finally in a long, long, long, long time see the result. But in reality, one simple action step can actually create a result right away, especially if it's resonant with who you are, and gives you that "I think I'm gonna puke" feeling

## YOUR NEXT STEP!

It's really important to me that my clients get the opportunity to try things out and get a result while we're working together. Even during the course of my eight-week program, while we're co-creating a strategy together I challenge them to take an action that will generate a Result That Matters to them even before their full strategy is in place. In my experience, taking fast, resonant action is an amazing way to generate momentum, and it works for my clients over and over and over again.

So your mission, should you choose to accept it, is to decide what your next action step needs to be, and GO DO IT. Like right NOW. And the scarier and more resonant with you and your values it is, the better. (Remember, you want it to make you feel like you might puke to do it, but not like you'll want to punch yourself in the face over and over again for picking it as your tactic.)

Then, hop over to my free community for entrepreneurs, The Growth Tribe, and report back on how it's going. I love hearing about results, but if you need a little hand-holding (or maybe hair-holding, as it were) to get you through the vomit stage and ensure you actually do the scary thing, feel free to pop in there for some accountability and support as well. The link to join is: HustleFreeBusiness.com/toolkit. And please tag me in your post so I won't miss it and can cheer you on and hold your hair!

# CONCLUSION
# YOUR NEXT STEPS ...

*"All endings are also beginnings. We just don't know it at the time."*
*Mitch Albom*

*"Twenty years from now you will be more disappointed by the things you didn't do than by the ones you did. So throw off the bowlines. Sail away from the safe harbor. Catch the trade wind in your sails."*
*Mark Twain*

L ook at that. You made it!! You've reached the end of this book, my friend. Well done, you. If you've gotten this far and followed the RESULTS Rituals I shared it means that you've accomplished some amazing things. And it also means that you are a whole new person. Let's take a moment to really acknowledge all that you've done for yourself here.

• You recognized that the way you were working in your business and your life was unsustainable and not worth doing anymore so you laid down your hustle and released it, resistance be damned! Since you now know the difference between spirit resistance and fear-based resistance you're fully equipped to know what is likely to spark hustle mode and what to choose instead that will not only feel better and more fun to do, but will also generate ongoing exponential growth within you and your business.

- You decided that your Epic Mission was just too bloody important to go another day not getting after it so you got crystal clear on what it looked like and prioritized creating it. You allowed yourself to see all that was possible for you and for the world when you unlimit yourself and actually go after all that amazing potential out there. And you now know that not only can you bring it to life, but that you simply must.

- You connected to the successful person that exists within you who's already done the thing you're setting out to do and became her. You simultaneously hacked away the layers and layers and layers of stucco that hid that Golden Buddha within and Summoned Your Excellence. Because you're now so clear on your values and intentions, you know exactly what filter to use with every decision you make from here forward to ensure that they're resonant with who you are, what you want, and with the trajectory you're on for bringing your Epic Mission to life.

- You figured out that other people's formulas, blueprints, and roadmaps weren't your thing anymore, and that the best strategy you could ever follow was one that incorporated YOU into it. And then you created yours! A powerful plan that allows you to create the Results That Matter to you while actually enjoying yourself at the same time because it's infused with your values and intentions.

- You committed to your Epic Mission, to the people in the world who are counting on you to show up for them, to your values and intentions, and most importantly, to yourself. You also got a set of tools that ensures that you actually stand by those commitments going forward, since that's what really counts. And you realized that the growth and transformation that you really want, and that your Epic Mission needs from you, requires you to invest in yourself, no matter how scary it may seem to do it.

- You opened your eyes to Humanity's Biggest Lie and were simultaneously relieved to learn that you're not as alone as you thought you were in life. Then you started thinking about who you need to have in your life that will support, uplift, and challenge you to Summon Your Excellence every - single - day. You now know that you absolutely can't go it alone anymore if you want to create the change in the world you're here to create so you're on the hunt for a community that will have your back as you continue on your journey.

- And finally you actually took some action and created a result!! You saw that every action you take in your business can and should align with what's most important to you, and that those actions need nurturing and love, just like seeds in a vegetable garden do. And you realized that you could shortcut your activities and get results even faster by being willing to take action closer to the result and eliminate inefficiencies that probably felt like "shoulds" anyway. And finally you connected to the power of the puke factor and committed to taking as many vomit-worthy actions as possible because you know how powerful they are and how quickly they'll generate momentum and results for you, even if they do scare the bejezus out of you at first.

WOW. That is some amazing stuff you've just done. Take just a moment and let all of that settle in.

No, seriously. Do it. I'll wait…

Now that you've reached the end of this part of your journey, your next step is to actually **put your plan into action**. This is where the rubber meets the road and will likely be the scariest part of this evolution for you. Know going in that your demons will return, your inner committee will get noisy, and resistance will be there to try and convince you to do something else. Ultimately there are two opportunities that lay ahead of you. The reason I know this is because I've seen this fork in the road with every single one of my clients. And I've stood at this intersection before myself a few times in my life.

The path on the right will take you someplace just fine. You'll walk away from this book with your completed strategy in one hand and a fistful of good intentions in the other. You'll dive in with energy and vigor and start seeing results. You'll put "get support" or "find a community to connect with" on your to-do list but put it on hold for now while you "integrate everything" and figure "all this other stuff" out first. And then a week or two or maybe even less will pass by and your old habits will start to creep back in. You'll see someone post on Facebook about their $6 million launch, or an ad for some new blueprint, software, or social media tool will catch your eye, or someone's new course that promises to generate $100,000/month will start calling to you. And you'll drift. You'll wander right back to where you were when you started this book. Which is actually just fine, if it's where you consciously choose you're more comfortable being. You can pick up the ashen remains of that hustle badge, dust it off and put it right back on if that is what you know you want to do. But I encourage you to consciously choose it; don't just let it happen without realizing it. There's power in that choice, know that.

Or you can take the path on the left. On this path you walk away with the same strategy, and the same good intentions, but here your commitment actually finds roots. You create rituals to change your habits. You do the work you need to do to create the Results That Matter to you and actually **enjoy what you're doing.** You find opportunities every single day to Summon Your Excellence and BE the person who's already done the thing you're setting out to do. You find the support and community you need **immediately** to ensure you are seen and accountable and are actually doing those things each and every moment of the day. You start creating the Results That Matter to you quickly and with ease, and you let that momentum carry you along effortlessly. Your people start to change as you do, and you begin to get some real traction not only in your business, but also on your Epic Mission.

So which path will you take?

You know, I wrote this book because I didn't want one more person to go through life feeling like they can't or shouldn't or won't ever achieve their fullest potential. We haven't even met, and yet I can already see all that power, and Excellence, and grace inside of you from here. And the idea that you might not see it yourself, or worse yet, that you might not share it with the world absolutely kills me.

The world needs YOU!!! And not the small, meek you that second-guesses herself. The world needs that biggest, baddest, most amazing YOU that I can see in you. She exists already. And she's waiting patiently for you to invite her to come out and play. The world is DYING for you to do it. The time is now. No more waiting. No more hustling. No more confusion.

BE that you. Change the world. I promise with the RESULTS Rituals in your back pocket it will be effortless. When your possibilities are limitless, when you have a plan in place that resonates with who you are and what you value, and when you're surrounded by the support and momentum you need to succeed, you simply cannot fail. And I cannot wait to experience the new world you've already created that's lying in wait for you to bring it to life.

# ACKNOWLEDGEMENTS

T here are so many people I want to thank for the love and support they've provided that have brought me to this place in my journey. I am certain that I will leave off someone important, so I will apologize in advance for doing so.

To all of the entrepreneurial communities and leaders who've embraced me, loved me, lifted me up, and seen and reflected back my genius to me (and to the rest of the world!) I am forever grateful. Angela Lauria and the Order of the Quill, Giovanni Marsico and the Archangels, Darla LeDoux and the Aligned Entrepreneurs, Todd Herman and the original 90-Day Year Crew, Mike Dooley and the IPpies, Marie Forleo and the B-Schoolers, thank you for believing in me. You've lit my fire, stoked it to a raging inferno, and continue to fan the flames of my success. I would never have gotten here without all of you having my back.

To The Growth Tribe! My people! I love each of you so very much. How lucky am I to have drawn to me such an extraordinary group of world-changing entrepreneurs? Thank you for bringing your gifts to the Tribe (and to the world) every day. And thank you for giving me a reason to step up and be the leader I was born to be.

To Angela Lauria, Cynthia Kane, Heidi Miller, Mila Nedeljkov, and the rest of The Author Incubator crew, I cannot express in words the gratitude I feel having found you. Not only did I WRITE A EFFING BOOK but I got to change my life completely through the process. I'd call that a supreme win-win.

To the Morgan James Publishing team: Special thanks to David Hancock, CEO & Founder for believing in me and my message. To my Author Relations Manager, Gayle West, thanks for making the process seamless and easy. Many more thanks to everyone else, but especially Jim Howard, Bethany Marshall, and Nickcole Watkins.

To Team Awesome, my kick-ass book launch partners, for spreading the word and generating monumental excitement about my book and mission! You're aptly named because you're all so "awesome" to support me and help me get this book in front of the people who need it most.

To my beautiful, inspired, outrageously talented clients, Yola Mehmeti, Cindi Roberts, Jaime Drummond, Laura Franklin, Tonia Percy, Martine Metaxas, Anne-Marie MacNamara, Jeanette LeBlanc, and Suze Solari, you guys are simply amazing. I cannot believe how lucky I am that I get to work with such a talented group of people every day. And that I get to help you change the world with your Epic Missions? That's me fulfilling my life's purpose. Thank you for honoring me with the opportunity to do that.

To Kelly Sheets and Josh Leslie, my biz partners and biz besties. You two are the absolute BEST!! I'm not sure I've ever had a more authentic, genuine, creative, energetic, and committed cheerleading squad in my corner in the entire 40 years I've been on this planet. I hope that I am half the friend and partner to you two as you each continue to be to me. I aspire to see the world and dedicate myself to bettering it in the same ways each of you do. Thank you for completing my Trifecta of Awesome!

To my soul council, my best friends, the people who stand by me through all the ups and downs this crazy ride called "entrepreneurship" takes me on, Wendy Wolff, Trish Kapinos, Rebecca Niziol, Michelle Lowbridge, Annie Rodrigues, Sandra Luttrell, Megan Langston, Jeff Sanders and Danielle Watson, thank you for being my mirror of who I truly am, and all that is truly possible for me in this lifetime. I'm simultaneously inspired, driven, and awed by the love and greatness within each of you.

To my parents and sisters, Anne Hamilton, Bob Latzen, Lorrie Latzen, Ellen Latzen and Elena Latzen, thank you for always (ALWAYS) being there for me. For helping to mold who I am and who I will continue to become. I'm so lucky to have been born into this clan and am even more thrilled that August gets to grow up with each of your influence in her life as well.

To my baby girl, August, for being the greatest manifestation of an intention I've ever encountered. Your spirit, wisdom, love, and light at 14 months old are unlike anyone else on the planet. I am driven every single day to be the absolute best I can be, to make magic things happen in the world, to inspire others to do the same, and to be a powerful, successful woman so that you will know that it's all possible for you too. Thank you for choosing me, for bestowing me the greatest gift of my lifetime, to be your Mama.

And to Tom. You are simply remarkable. No matter how crazy and impractical my ideas may seem on the surface, you continue to jump on my bandwagon. You see the potential in me and remind me of it when I forget. You are the best partner in parenting EVER. And you make food appear as if from nowhere. Thank you for simply being YOU. And for simply loving ME.

# ABOUT THE AUTHOR

A my Birks can see the future. No, she doesn't use a crystal ball or some time travel device. Amy was born with the ability to see the biggest, brightest, most vibrant potential in everyone and everything she encounters. Known as The Strategy Ninja, she uses her GPS brain to help mission-driven, heart-centered coaches grow their businesses and get the results that matter to them FAST, and with fun, ease and purpose. Often referred to as a "master connector", Amy's 10 years of corporate strategy and project management experience make her the purposeful coach's secret weapon for growth and results. She lives in the beautiful Central Coast of California with her husband Tom, daughter August, and pup Maynard, who regularly indulge her love of old school hip hop and impromptu kitchen dance parties.

Amy loves new connections! Here's where to find her:

www.AmyBirks.com

www.facebook.com/amylatzenbirks

Instagram: @amy.birks
Twitter: @AmyBBirks
Ninja@amybirks.com

# THANK YOU

My friend, you've reached the end of the book! Congratulations on your commitment to your business, your growth, and most importantly yourself. To ensure you get the most out of this book and the strategy you'll create with it, I've put together a bundle of FREE resources for you, many of which I referred to in the book. All you have to do to access my Hustle-Free Business Toolkit is to visit HustleFreeBusiness.com/toolkit. Enjoy!

## YOUR HUSTLE-FREE BUSINESS TOOLKIT INCLUDES:

- An invitation to attend my free Hustle-Free Fridays LIVE weekly training series

- Release Your Hustle Video Training

  - If you've ever thought, "there's got to be a better way!" this video training is for you. In this short, 5-minute video I guide you through an in-depth process to Release Your Hustle once and for all

- Summon Your Excellence Mini-Course
  - In this 15-minute mini-course I walk through:
    - Exactly how to define your Excellence
    - A process to help you identify what triggers you **not** being in your Excellence now
    - A framework for avoiding those triggers so you can be in your Excellence **all the time**
    - The power of role models
    - And more!

- Uncover Your Strategy Master Class
  - If you're anything like the majority of my clients you've probably thought to yourself, "I wish someone would just tell me the steps to follow so I can go do them!" Well, this Master Class will do just that, but you'll create your strategy custom to meet your individual needs!
  - This recorded class walks you through my strategic planning process step by step and will help ensure you craft the best possible strategy for YOU.

- Declaration Statement Worksheet
  - If you prefer a PDF to an exercise in the book, I've created a worksheet to help you craft the most kick-ass Declaration Statement ever to make those commitments of yours unbreakable!

- Magic Leaf Video
    - In chapter 7 I shared a story about some magic showing up for me. Here's the video proof of what happened

- The Growth Tribe
    - I would LOVE for you to join my community of heart-centered, mission-driven entrepreneurs! It's free, and amazing.

- Inspiration on the Go
    - I put together a list of my favorite books, podcasts, and other resources for getting inspired in a hurry. I know you'll love it!

# Morgan James
# Speakers Group

*www.TheMorganJamesSpeakersGroup.com*

We connect Morgan James published
authors with live and online events
and audiences who will benefit
from their expertise.

Printed in the USA
CPSIA information can be obtained
at www.ICGtesting.com
JSHW082357140824
68134JS00020B/2116